THE

CELTIC WAY

OF PRAYER

THE

CELTIC WAY
OF PRAYER

ESTHER DE WAAL

DOUBLEDAY
New York London Toronto Sydney Auckland

PUBLISHED BY DOUBLEDAY
a division of Bantam Doubleday Dell Publishing Group, Inc.
1540 Broadway, New York, New York 10036

DOUBLEDAY and the portrayal of an anchor with a dolphin are
trademarks of Doubleday, a division of
Bantam Doubleday Dell Publishing Group, Inc.

Book design by Bonni Leon-Berman

Library of Congress Cataloging-in-Publication Data
De Waal, Esther.
The Celtic way of prayer / Esther de Waal. — 1st ed.
p.   cm.
Includes bibliographical references and index.
1. Celtic Church.   2. Celts—Religion.   3. Prayer—
Christianity.   4. Spiritual life—Christianity.   I. Title.
BR748.D4   1997
299'.16—dc20   96-19712
CIP
ISBN 0-385-48663-4
August 1997
First Edition
1   3   5   7   9   10   8   6   4   2

CONTENTS

Acknowledgments

I should like to acknowledge with great gratitude permissions from the following:

Trustees of the Scottish Academic Press for permission to quote so widely from the *Carmina Gadelica* Vol. I & II.

Fr. Noel Dermott O'Donoghue and T & T Clark Publishers for the new rendering of "St. Patrick's Breastplate."

Dr. Oliver Davies and Dr. Fiona Bowie and SPCK, for the recent translations of early Welsh material taken from their anthology *Celtic Christian Spirituality.*

Thomas Owen Clancy & Gilbert Markus and The Edinburgh University Press for the lines from the "Altus Prosator" and verses from "Cantemus in Mon Dei" from *Iona, the Earliest Poetry of a Celtic Monastery.*

Cynthia and Saunders Davies and The Church of Wales Publications for Euros Bowen's poem "Gloria."

Gillian Clarke and Carcanet for a few lines from her poem "Fires on Llyn."

INTRODUCTION

THE REDISCOVERY OF the Celtic world has been an extraordinary revelation for many Christians in recent years, an opening up of the depths and riches within our own tradition that many of us had not before suspected. As I reflect on what it has meant to me, I think that above all it has enriched my understanding of prayer. It has taught me, and encouraged me into, a deeper, fuller way of prayer. I have come to see that the Celtic way of prayer is prayer with the whole of myself, a totality of praying that embraces the fullness of my own personhood, and allows me not only to pray with words but also, more important, with the heart, the feelings, using image and symbol, touching the springs of my imagination.

I like to think of it as a journey into prayer. The Celtic understanding of journeying is in itself so rich and so significant. It is *peregrinatio*, seeking, quest, adventure, wandering, exile—it is ultimately a journey, as I try to show in the first chapter, to find the place of my resurrection, the resurrected self, the self that I might hope to be, to become, the true self in Christ. This journey is possible only because I am finding my roots—that familiar paradox known in all monastic life and a reflection of basic human experience, that only if one is rooted at home in one's own self, in the place in which one finds oneself, is one able to move forward, to open up new boundaries, both exterior and interior, in other words, to embark on a life of continual and never-ending conversion, transformation. To find my roots takes me back to the part of my self that is more ancient than I am, and this is, of course, the power of the Celtic heritage. In my own case there are both my family roots, which are Scottish, and the place where I was born, and where I now once again live, which is the Border country of Wales. But for any of us the Celtic tradition is the ancient or elemental—a return to the elements, the earth, stone, fire, water, the ebb and flow of tides and seasons, the pattern of the year as it swings on its axis from Samhaine, November 1, when all grows dark, to Beltaine, May 1, the coming of light and spring. To pray the Celtic way means above all to be aware of this rhythm of dark and light. The dark and the light are themselves symbols of the Celtic refusal to deny darkness, pain, suffering and yet to exult in rejoicing, celebration in the fullness and goodness of life. This is in itself a recognition of the fullness of my own humanity.

Coming from the farthest fringes of the Western world, Celtic Christianity (an expression I prefer to use rather than speaking of the Celtic Church)[1] keeps alive what is ancient Christian usage, usage which like that of the East comes from a deep central point before the Papacy began to tidy up and to rationalize. This was more difficult in Ireland, Scotland, and Wales, the Isle of Man, Cornwall and Brittany, the main Celtic areas, simply because of geographical distance and the lack of towns. This point is of more than antiquarian interest: It also speaks to me symbolically, taking me back to the ancient, the early, both in my own self, and in the experience of Christendom, where I encounter something basic, primal, fundamental, universal. I am taken back beyond the party labels and the denominational divisions of the Church today, beyond the divides of the Reformation or the schism of East and West. I am also taken beyond the split of intellect and feeling, of mind and heart, that came with the growth of the rational and analytical approach that the development of the universities brought to the European mind in the twelfth century. Here is something very profound. This deep point within the Christian tradition touches also some deep point in my own consciousness, my own deepest inner self.

This tapestry of the riches of the Celtic way of prayer has about it something of the variety of shapes and colors that I find in a page of the *Book of Kells,* and so I find myself asking where and how we can begin to unravel one of these extraordinary spirals or threads so that it leads us on into our exploration. I think that the essential starting point is the fact that Celtic Christianity was essentially monastic, as indeed the origins of Christianity in the whole of Britain were strictly monastic.[2] The Celtic way of prayer was learned from the monasteries; it was from its religious communities that the people learned to pray. As a result, they learned that there was no separation of praying and living; praying and working flow into each other, so that life is to be punctuated by prayer, become prayer. If ordinary people took their ideas on prayer from this ideal of continual prayer, it should not really surprise us that when we uncover something of the way of praying that was handed down in the oral tradition and was collected in Scotland

and Ireland at the end of the last century, what we find is lay spirituality, a household religion in which praying is inseparable from an ordinary daily working life.[3]

Those earliest years in Ireland and Wales forged a powerful mix between monastic Christianity and what existed already in the people to whom this Christian message was now brought. It was the way in which Christianity responded to what it found in these lands that gives it its unique character and emphasis. The Celtic countries lay on the edge of the known Western world, largely outside the Roman Empire, a people lacking the social molds and mental framework and cultural infrastructure the Roman Empire brought elsewhere. These were a rural people, living close to the earth, close to stone and water, and their religious worship was shaped by their awareness of these elemental forces. They were a rural people for whom the clan, the tribe, and kinship were important, a close-knit people who thought of themselves in a corporate way as belonging to one another. They were a warrior people, a people whose myths and legends told them of heroes and heroic exploits. Above all, they were a people of the imagination, whose amazing artistic achievements in geometric design, filigree work, and enameling can be seen in La Tène art, and whose skill with words (spoken not written) flowered in poetry and storytelling. This was a society in which the poet held a highly respected place, played a professional role, and where storytelling was taken seriously and demanded many years of study and learning. All this was taken up by a Christianity that was not afraid of what it found but felt that it was natural to appropriate it into the fullness of Christian living and praying. So the Celtic way of prayer is a reflection of this: It is elemental, corporate, heroic, imaginative. This is its gift to us.

As I have gone deeper in my exploration of the Celtic heritage, I have found that it has touched me profoundly at many levels that had not hitherto been a familiar part of my twentieth-century upbringing and education. I discovered that if I wanted to encounter Celtic Christianity, I had to look at poetry, and so I found myself being taken into the world of poetry and song. My own religious upbringing had been so intellectual and cerebral, a matter of going to church, of reciting the Creed, of saying prayers. And instead here was a world that told me books were not enough, that books could not express the wonder of the world that God had made:

> The Father created the world by a miracle;
> it is difficult to express its measure.
> Letters cannot contain it, letters cannot
>   comprehend it.[4]

The Celtic journey that I am describing in this book is unlike any other journey I know. Its shape and its end are different, as are the songs I sing while I journey, the company I keep along the road. I have been brought into contact with the visual and the nonverbal, confronted by the power of image and of symbol. I have found myself thinking about God as a poet, an artist, drawing us all into his great work of art. I have been taken beyond the rational and intellectual and cerebral, for this world touches the springs of my imagination. I am reminded of what Thomas Merton said in *Contemplation in a World of Action* about the role of the imagination as a discovering faculty, as a means of seeing new meanings, and above all as an essential element in prayer:

> Imagination is the creative task of making symbols, joining things together in such a way that they throw new light on each other and on everything around them. The imagination is a discovering faculty, a faculty for seeing relationships, for seeing meanings that are special and even quite new. The imagination is something which enables us to discover unique present meaning in a given moment of our life. Without imagination the contemplative life can be extremely dull and fruitless.[5]

So I have been brought face-to-face with a world at once very familiar and very mysterious, for I have found in the Celtic a worldview that touches on much that is common, shared, perhaps archetypal, in all human experience. I have become aware of how this way of seeing the world is common to all early peoples, to the traditional and aboriginal peoples throughout the world. Although I do not develop it here, I am sure that the exploration of this Celtic world will be prophetic for the future as we try to break down the barriers so that we may reach out to one another. This discovery of my own Celtic roots has meant that I have also become more aware of the riches of many other traditional peoples. I have found that much in the African or Native

American experience speaks the same language as the Celtic, has a shared and common resonance. For I have found in Celtic understanding nothing of the highly individualistic, competitive, inward-looking approach common in today's society. Here, instead, everyone sees themselves in relation to one another, and that extends beyond human beings to the wild creatures, the birds and the animals, the earth itself.[6] This has brought a sense of being a part of the whole web of being. There is something here of "the breathing together of all things" as Teilhard de Chardin put it, something of the mystery of coinherence of which Charles Williams writes in his novels. The new science speaks much the same language, of mutual interdependence. Here is the promise of a more holistic approach to the world, of healing of the many fractures that maim and corrupt each of us and the world in which we live.

The Celtic world touches all of this but yet remains totally unique, earthy, and mysterious, knowing darkness and pain but equally rejoicing in light, full of poetry and song and celebration, showing me the depths of penitence and the heights of praise, touching me in the secret hidden parts of my own self and yet connecting me with others. So although each of us is in the end solitary (and that is something that Celtic Christianity knows well), I am reminded that I travel in company with those who have made this *peregrinatio* before me, by the whole company of heaven, the saints and the angels, a "cloud of witnesses," who surround me and who hold me up as I go.

THE

CELTIC WAY

OF PRAYER

1

JOURNEYING

THE WHOLE IDEA of the journey is basic to humanity. I think of the universality of the image of the quest, the myths of the odyssey or the search for the Holy Grail, the many stories of wandering and exodus. The monastic life has always been that of continual conversion, moving on, the never-ending transformation of the old into the new. Jung's psychic reality is journeying on. If we say yes to Christ's call to follow him, our Christian discipleship asks of us to follow a man who had nowhere to lay his head. Christ himself is the Way and his followers are people of the Way. Just as he entered the wilderness, like Moses and the children of Israel, and made his own journey through life to death and resurrection and new life, so that pattern is inescapable for us all. And if in this model we see Christ encountering temptation and hardship, we, his followers, should not expect anything less. This journey will be costly and the Celtic tradition never allows us to forget just how costly. It is also surprising and risky, not necessarily following any clear-cut pattern of having some end and goal in view so that the purpose can be clearly established and then followed. For the really significant journey is the interior journey. As Dag Hammarskjöld said, "The longest journey is the journey inward." It is here that I need help, and this is one of the reasons why I have found it such a source of

1

strength and inspiration on my own journey to look at the Celtic understanding of *peregrinatio,* a word and concept that is found nowhere else in Christendom.

The word itself is almost untranslatable, but its essence is caught in the ninth-century story of three Irishmen drifting over the sea from Ireland for seven days, in coracles without oars, coming ashore in Cornwall and then being brought to the court of King Alfred. When he asked them where they had come from and where they were going they answered that they "stole away because we wanted for the love of God to be on pilgrimage, we cared not where." This wonderful response and this amazing undertaking comes out of the inspirational character of early Irish spirituality. It shows at once how misleading is that word "pilgrimage" as we use it and how very different indeed is the Celtic *peregrinatio* from the pilgrimages of the Middle Ages or the present day. There is no specific end or goal such as that of reaching a shrine or a holy place that allows the pilgrim at the end of the journey to return home with a sense of a mission accomplished. *Peregrinatio* is not undertaken at the suggestion of some monastic abbot or superior but because of an inner prompting in those who set out, a passionate conviction that they must undertake what was essentially an inner journey. Ready to go wherever the Spirit might take them, seeing themselves as *hospites mundi,* "guests of the world," what they are seeking is the place of their resurrection, the resurrected self, the true self in Christ, which is for all of us our true home.

So *peregrinatio* presents us with the ideal of the interior, inward journey that is undertaken for the love of God, or for the love of Christ, *pro amore Christi*. The impulse is love. And if the journey is undertaken for the love of Christ, then it argues that Christ must already hold a place in our lives.

> *To go to Rome*
> *Is much of trouble, little of profit;*
> *The King whom thou seekest there,*
> *Unless thou bring Him with thee, thou wilt*
> * not find.*[1]

This short poem reminds me of a truth I must never forget: I shall not find Christ at the end of the journey unless he accompanies me along the way. The same idea is expressed in a saying attributed to the wise saint Samthann of Clonbroney, who is reputed to have told the hermit who wanted to look for God in foreign lands: "Were God to be found overseas, I too would take ship and go. But since God is near to all that call upon him, there is no constraint upon us to seek him overseas. For from every land there is a way to the kingdom of Heaven."[2]

"Let us not love the roadway rather than the homeland lest we lose our eternal home; for we have such a home that we ought to love it," wrote St. Columbanus, one of the greatest of all *peregrini*. At the end of the sixth century, already middle-aged, he had set out to wander over the face of Europe and was finally to die at Bobbio in Italy in 615. "Therefore let this principle abide with us, that on the road we live as travellers, as pilgrims, as guests of the world . . .

singing with grace and power, 'When shall I come and appear before the face of my God?' "[3]

In those words "guests of the world" St. Columbanus has given me a phrase I treasure on my journey. In a later sermon he says "the end of the road is the end of our life, the end of our roadway is our home" and that again brings me back to the theme of "the place of resurrection." I am reminded of Bairre of Cork, who traveled with an angel guiding him who would say at a certain place, "Not here shall be thy resurrection," until finally they reached the place where Cork stands today and then at last he said, "Abide here, for here shall be thy haven of resurrection." "The haven of thy resurrection" is another of these small phrases that I hold in my hand, as it were, and feel its weight and enjoy the richness of its meaning.[4]

However passionate the desire and however total the commitment, this way of *peregrinatio* is bound to be costly. It means becoming a stranger and an exile to all that is familiar, safe. But the *peregrini* found an example in Christ, who willingly came down from heaven and so they could look toward him and see that voluntary exile is laudable since it is in imitation of Christ himself.[5]

It is an exile that demands the stripping of family and possessions, the rooting out from heart and mind of all one's own aims and desires. The great Celtic scholar Gougaud used to point out that God's command to Abraham always seemed to have had a special appeal to the Irish people as a call from God to sacrifice what was most dear to them. It is to take the words "Go forth" addressed to Abraham as words addressed to one's own self. St. Columba is reputed to have said in a sermon:

> *God counseled Abraham to leave his own country*
> *and go in pilgrimage into the land which God had*
> *shown him, to wit the "Land of Promise"—Now the*
> *good counsel which God enjoined here on the father*
> *of the faithful is incumbent on all the faithful; that is*
> *to leave their country and their land, their wealth*
> *and their worldly delight for the sake of the Lord of*
> *the Elements, and go in perfect pilgrimage in*
> *imitation of Him.*[6]

St. Columba, of course, in leaving Ireland for Scotland, knew exile only too well. He felt so deeply the pain of parting from his native country that he could say "the great cry of the people of Doire has broken my heart in four." And sitting on the headland of Iona, looking across the straits at the land from which he is now exiled, a poem that is ascribed to him speaks of what that parting has cost him. He writes with a depth of sadness of what he is leaving behind, for it is not only his earthly kin, family and friends, and the warmth and security of the small, close-knit community that bonded them, it is also the nonhuman, the land itself, nature, each leaf of the oaks he has known and loved, and not least the angels, of which Derry is full. So he says farewell to his native monastic home and makes his way toward the isles of Alba, the early Scotland:

Great is the speed of my coracle,
And its stern turned upon Derry;
Grievous is my errand over the main,
Travelling to Alba of the beetling brows.

Were all Alba mine
From its centre to its border,
I would rather have the site of a house
In the middle of fair Derry.

It is for this I love Derry,
For its smoothness, for its purity;
All full of angels
Is every leaf on the oaks of Derry.

My Derry, my little oak-grove,
My dwelling and my little cell,
O living God that art in Heaven above,
Woe to him who violates it![7]

"The path I walk, Christ walks it." The opening words of a traditional poem attributed to St. Columba ask for the protection and support of Christ's presence on this journey wherever it may carry us.

> *The path I walk, Christ walks it. May the land in*
> *which I am be without sorrow.*
> *May the Trinity protect me wherever I stay, Father,*
> *Son, and Holy Spirit.*

Bright angels walk with me—dear presence—in every
   dealing.
In every dealing I pray them that no one's poison
   may reach me.
The ninefold people of heaven of holy cloud, the
   tenth force of the stone earth.
Favourable company, they come with me, so that the
   Lord may not be angry with me.
May I arrive at every place, may I return home; may
   the way in which I spend be a way without loss.
May every path before me be smooth, man, woman
   and child welcome me.
A truly good journey! Well does the fair Lord show
   us a course, a path.[8]

Thomas Merton, in teaching his novices at Gethsemani what they might expect from their monastic vocation, also used Abraham as the exemplar of a life that he saw as a journey, leaving home in search of God. By becoming a monk, he wrote, "one becomes a stranger, an exile. We go into the midst of the unknown, we live on earth as strangers." So in a poem he can, like St. Columba, write of his own experience of exile.

We are exiles in the far end of solitude, living as
   listeners,
With hearts attending to the skies we cannot
   understand:

*Waiting upon the first far drums of Christ the
Conqueror,
Planted like sentinels upon the world's frontier.*[9]

*By thinking nothing of the place of his birth, by
forsaking his own land, he sought to find it; by living
in exile he hoped to reach home.*[10]

The Welsh saint of the fifth century, St. Brynach, who had
his church at Nevern in Pembrokeshire, in speaking of
"home" adds one more vital word to my understanding of
the journey of the *peregrini:* the need to find a home, to be
at home, in all the many levels that that word can carry. For
to be earthed and grounded in the reality of being at home
in one's own self and in the world around touches on something that is essential, necessary, if my journey is to have a
form and shape. The apparent freedom and abandonment
of the early Celtic world could give a misleading impression
if it were ever to be mistaken for restless wandering. It is
true that the early Celtic monastic rules, written in verse,
unsystematic, concerned with the spirit rather than with
practical detail, are very different from the orderly monastic
rules of the West, such as the Rule of St. Benedict. It is also
true that the early Celtic monastic sites randomly scattered,
pluriform, proliferating, have the generous character of being wide-open cities that welcome all, monastic and lay
alike. *"Amor non tenet ordinam"*—love does not concern
itself with order—as St. Columbanus once said in a letter
defending his own spontaneous, free-flowing style. But I
need to remember that in all of this there is a sense of

underlying purpose, an awareness of the importance of form and structure. Those like the tinkers whose journeys are meaningless are held in disfavor. Legend carried on in oral tradition has this story to tell: that at the time of the Crucifixion, when Christ was brought to the cross and when no nails could be found, a tinker woman blew up the fire and made the nails. And Christ, nailed on the tree, said to the tinker woman who was standing there at its foot, "Thou and thy kind from generation to generation, from age to age, shall be walking the ways and travelling the wilderness, without rest of night, without peace of day, because of the work of thy hand and thine ill deed."[11] I am reminded of what St. Benedict has to say when he castigates the gyrovag, the aimless wanderer, the person who is never at rest but goes on continually seeking, drifting, living off other people, hoping for something new. This is not the Celtic way, and the openness of the *peregrinatio* should never tempt me to forget that without the still center, the journey, whether inner or outer, is impossible.

We find in the *Carmina Gadelica* the poems, songs, prayers, and blessings, handed down orally from generation to generation, of a people who had a very strong sense of the journey in all its aspects. The whole of life itself is for them a journey from birth to death; there are the short daily journeys that are a part of their working life as they go about their ordinary and mundane tasks; and there are the longer journeys, when men and women leave home or leave the country. So the journey and the life itself are one whole. When the time came for Alexander Carmichael to leave the

Isles, he went to say good-bye to all the people whom he had come to know and one of them, Mor MacNeill, who was "poor and old and alone" sent him on his way with words that always seem to me to reveal totally unselfconsciously the holistic way of seeing the world out of which the "journey-prayers" grow.

> And you are now going away and leaving your people and your country, dear one of my heart! Well, then, whole may you be, and well may it go with you, every way you go and every step you travel. And my own blessing go with you, and the blessing of God go with you, and the blessing of the Mary Mother go with you, every time you rise up and every time you lie down, until you lie down in sleep upon the arm of Jesus Christ of the virtues and of the blessings.[12]

During his travels, Alexander Carmichael collected many beautiful journey-prayers and blessings of which this, from Ann Mackinnon, a crofter on the island of Coll, is typical:

> *The Gospel of the God of life*
> *To shelter thee, to aid thee;*
> *Yea, the Gospel of the beloved Christ*
> *The holy Gospel of the Lord;*

> *To keep thee from all malice,*
> *From every dole and dolour;*
> *To keep thee from all spite,*
> *From evil eye and anguish.*

Thou shalt travel thither, thou shalt travel hither,
  Thou shalt travel hill and headland,
Thou shalt travel down, thou shalt travel up,
  Thou shalt travel ocean and narrow.

Christ Himself is shepherd over thee,
  Enfolding thee on every side;
He will not forsake thee hand or foot
  Nor let evil come anigh thee.[13]

The journey blessing that comes from Mary MacDonald, a crofter on South Uist, has a sense of the presence of the Trinity accompanying the traveler, that profound and totally natural experience of God as Trinity that is so much a mark of Celtic prayer:

God be with thee in every pass,
Jesus be with thee on every hill,
Spirit be with thee on every stream,
  Headland and ridge and lawn;

Each sea and land, each moor and meadow,
Each lying down, each rising up,
In the trough of the waves, on the crest of the
  billows,
  Each step of the journey thou goest.[14]

At the start of his journey the traveler asks a blessing for himself, thinking of the strangers whom he will meet on the road and how he will need the love of Christ, both to

give and to receive, as he faces the unknown places that lie
ahead. Carmichael tells us that his family and friends would
start out with him and join in its singing.

> *Life be in my speech,*
> *Sense in what I say,*
> *The bloom of cherries on my lips,*
> *Till I come back again.*
>
> *The love Christ Jesus gave*
> *Be filling every heart for me,*
> *The love Christ Jesus gave*
> *Filling me for every one.*
>
> *Traversing corries, traversing forests,*
> *Traversing valleys long and wild*
> *The fair white Mary still uphold me*
> *The Shepherd Jesu be my shield,*
> *The fair white Mary still uphold me,*
> *The Shepherd Jesu be my shield.*[15]

When a son or daughter was leaving home in the Western
Isles, friends and neighbors came to say farewell, to bring
gifts and to pray for peace and prosperity in the adopted
land. An old blind woman in Uist told Carmichael, "By the
Book, love, you would not seek but listen to them although
your own heart were full and overflowing and you striving
to keep down the tears." Before crossing the threshold of
the old home, a parting hymn would be sung or chanted or
intoned or recited in slow, measured cadences:

The benison of God be to thee,
The benison of Christ be to thee,
The benison of Spirit be to thee,
And to thy children,
    To thee and to thy children.

The peace of God be to thee,
The peace of Christ be to thee,
The peace of Spirit be to thee,
During all thy life,
    All the days of thy life.

The keeping of God upon thee in every pass,
The shielding of Christ upon thee in every path,
The bathing of Spirit upon thee in every stream,
    In every land and sea thou goest.[16]

Another traditional custom when a member of a family was leaving home, whether for a short time or forever, was that the one who was leaving would bathe their face in warm milk (preferably in sheep's milk, as the sheep was sacred to Christ), since bathing represented purification and since during the flight into Egypt Mary had bathed her son:

The love that Mary gave to her one Son
    May all the world give me;
The love that Jesus gave to John Baptist
    Grant that I give to whoso meets me,

May the Son of God be at the outset of my journey,
    May the Son of God be in surety to aid me;
May the Son of God make clear my way,
    May the Son of God be at the end of my
        seeking.[17]

And then comes this most lovely blessing of all, that from a
mother to her children. It is full of warmth and tenderness,
and shows her most natural desire for the protection and
presence of God in their lives—just as I am sure that she
knew it in her own life, for how else could she speak, except
out of her own experience.

The joy of God in thy face,
    Joy to all who see thee,
The circle of God around thy neck,
    Angels of God shielding thee,
    Angels of God shielding thee.
Joy of night and day be thine,
Joy of sun and moon be thine,
Joy of men and women be thine,
    Each land and sea thou goest,
    Each land and sea thou goest.

Be every season happy for thee,
Be every season bright for thee,
Be every season glad for thee,
    And the Son of Mary Virgin at peace with thee,
    The Son of Mary Virgin at peace with thee.

Be thine the compassing of the God of life,
Be thine the compassing of the Christ of love,
Be thine the compassing of the Spirit of Grace,
    To befriend thee and to aid thee,
    Thou beloved one of my heart.[18]

And here is one finally that has come to mean much to me personally as I try to let my own sons go in freedom, lines that were apparently whispered by a mother in the ears of sons or daughters when they left home. I particularly love the almost physical sense of the protecting power of God that comes in that first line:

Be the great God between thy two shoulders
To protect thee in thy going and in thy coming,
Be the Son of Mary Virgin near thine heart,
And be the perfect Spirit upon thee pouring—
Oh, the perfect Spirit upon thee pouring![19]

But journeys are not made alone. They are made in the company of the saints and the angels, the members of the Trinity, and Mary, as this Irish blessing shows.

In the name of the Father with victory
And of the Son who suffered pain
That Mary and her Son may be with me on
    my travel.

O Mary meet me at the port
Do not let my soul go by Thee
Great is my fear at thy Son.

In the communion of the saints may we be
Listening to the voices of the angels
And praising the Son of God for ever and ever.[20]

So journey-prayers and blessings are an intrinsic part of life, to be crooned or recited to oneself whenever one left home, however small the errand, however short the distance, for men and women said that they always derived comfort from them. In these very short poems we can see how deeply this way of praying was woven into their lives.

Bless to me, O God,
  The earth beneath my foot
Bless to me, O God,
  The path whereon I go.[21]

Or again,

I on Thy path O God
Thou O God, in my steps.[22]

There is here not only a sense of the presence of God accompanying them wherever they may be, but also a sense of connectedness with the earth itself. These simple lines from an anonymous eleventh-century Welsh writer have always moved me:

Guard for me my feet
upon the gentle earth of Wales.

As I place my feet upon the earth, is it not a shared, reciprocal relationship? I treat the ground with reverence, but the ground also nurtures me. The Celtic way of seeing the world never lets me forget my relationship with the earth. For the Celtic peoples, God is "the Lord of the Elements" the name that St. Columba gave him. The strong sense of creation and of the presence of the Creator, of the unity that binds together heaven and earth, of men and women and the nonhuman, is something to which I am drawn back time and again, and for which I remain profoundly grateful.

Perhaps there is no more glorious expression of this than in St. Patrick's breastplate. The breastplate, or lorica, form of prayer is an ancient one, a protection prayer, a shield for a journey. Originally Druidic in usage, it was taken over, as so often happened, by the early Christian settlers of Ireland and put to Christian account. According to tradition, on Holy Saturday in the year 433 St. Patrick kindled the paschal fire on the hill of Slane which looked across to Tara, the center of the country and the seat of the High-King Laeghaire. The high-king was about to hold a festival in which all the lights and fires in the country were to be extinguished, and then he would light his fire, a ritual proclamation showing that only he and he alone would provide his people with light and fire. St. Patrick's fire was therefore a challenge to his ascendancy, and his wise men warned that unless this rival fire was put out immediately, it would flood the whole country with its light and burn until doomsday. A similar story is told of St. David, that when he took possession of the land, to the dismay of the local chieftain, and lit a fire, it was said: "the kindler of that fire shall excel all in powers and renown in every part that the smoke of his sacrifice has covered, even to the end of the world." Or St. Ciaran, the sixth-century Irish saint who founded one of the greatest of all early Irish monasteries, Clonmacnois. He lit a fire as he traveled, whereupon the watching pagans exclaimed: "the purpose for which yon fire is kindled tonight is such that it will never be put out."[23]

At the sight of this fire which threatened his power and authority, the high-king ordered St. Patrick to appear before him. So robed in white and with his companions, St. Patrick set out, chanting the Easter litanies and "a hymn in Irish invoking God's power and that of all his blessed creatures to protect them against the powers of evil and the spells and cruelties of heathendom" on this dangerous journey. The high-king laid ambush, but all that he saw was a group of deer and a fawn following them and for this reason the lorica is also known as "the deer's cry."

I

For my shield this day
  A mighty power:
  The Holy Trinity!
  Affirming threeness,
  Confessing oneness,
  In the making of all
  Through love . . .

II

For my shield this day I call:
Christ's power in his coming
and in his baptising,
Christ's power in his dying
On the cross, his arising
from the tomb, his ascending;
Christ's power in his coming
for judgment and ending.

III

For my shield this day I call:
strong power of the seraphim,
with angels obeying,
and archangels attending,
in the glorious company
of the holy and risen ones,
in the prayers of the fathers,
in visions prophetic
and commands apostolic,
in the annals of witness,
in virginal innocence,
to the deeds of steadfast men.

IV

For my shield this day I call:
Heaven's might,
Moon's whiteness,

Fire's glory,
Lightning's swiftness,
Wind's wildness,
Ocean's depth,
Earth's solidity,
Rock's immobility.

V

This day I call to me;
  God's strength to direct me,
  God's power to sustain me.
  God's wisdom to guide me,
  God's vision to light me,
  God's ear to my hearing,
  God's word to my speaking,
  God's hand to uphold me,
  God's pathway before me,
  God's shield to protect me,
  God's legions to save me:
  from snares of the demons,
  from evil enticements,
  from failings of nature,
  from one man or many
  that seek to destroy me,
  anear or afar.

VI

Around me I gather:
  these forces to save
  my soul and my body

from dark powers that assail me:
against false prophesyings,
against pagan devisings,
against heretical lying
and false gods all around me.
Against spells cast by women,
by blacksmiths, by Druids,
against knowledge unlawful
that injures the body,
that injures the spirit.

VII

Be Christ this day my strong protector:
against poison and burning
against drowning and wounding,
through reward wide and plenty . . .
Christ beside me, Christ before me;
Christ behind me, Christ within me;
Christ beneath me, Christ above me;
Christ to right of me, Christ to left of me;
Christ in my lying, my sitting, my rising;
Christ in heart of all who know me,
Christ on tongue of all who meet me,
Christ in eye of all who see me,
Christ in ear of all who hear me.

VIII

For my shield this day I call:
a mighty power:
the Holy Trinity!

affirming threeness,
confessing oneness
in the making of all—through love . . .

IX

For to the Lord belongs salvation,
and to the Lord belongs salvation
and to Christ belongs salvation.

May your salvation, Lord, be
with us always,
(Domini est salus, Domini est salus,
Christi est salus,
Salus tua, Domine, sit semper nobiscum.)[24]

When I read the breastplate and make it my own prayer on
my journey, I find that while it is a desperate entreaty, a cry
for help, it also carries a great feeling of confidence that the
powers that I invoke will come to my aid. And while I call
upon the majesty of the Creator God and all the forces of
the angelic hosts of heaven, I also call upon the tenderness
and the nearness of the person of Christ. So in the lorica I
swing between the two poles of distance and immediacy,
between the God who is remote and awesome and the God
whom I can actually touch and feel and who is immediately
close to me.

But it is the sheer glory of this great hymn that so
excites me! I know of nothing else which, so superbly, se-
renely, and yet energetically, can throw the whole universe
onto one canvas! In it I am given a tremendous credal affir-

mation of the unity of the universe and of men and women within it. It begins with the invocation of the Trinity and then it works its way through all the powers, through angels and archangels, through patriarchs and prophets and apostles, and so to sun and moon, fire, wind, sea, earth and rock, until finally there is each one of us created, surrounded by Christ. It feels as though it is woven in the same way as the Celtic strapwork on the carvings of the high crosses or the intricate pages of decoration of illuminated manuscripts, so that all the elements flow into one strong, gently unified harmony. Here is a powerful sense of the unity of the whole created order, a celebration of creation and redemption, that healing wholeness, the oneness in plurality that has always been so important a gift of the Celtic world to the fullness of my Christian understanding.

Of course I need protection from the powers of darkness, and the lorica has much to say about facing the dark forces. I am grateful that I find here no easy optimism that would deny the dark forces of a fallen world. The bland assurance that all is well is simply not true of the world that I know today, the world of war and famine and cruelty and injustice and AIDS and cancer as well as the no less destructive realities of poverty and economic hardship and unemployment. While there is a rejoicing in creation, it is never at the expense of any denial of the brokenness of the world. But there is always hope. The texts of early Celtic Christianity such as this come out of a confidence in the grace and mercy of God and his power to save a fallen world.[25]

I also know that often what I need is simply the energy to keep going, help to carry me along in times of tiredness, grayness, apathy, and drift. Here, in the very form of the words themselves and in the texture of the verses, I find that I am given the sense of a vibrant and life-giving force into which I can tap. The high-king might light his fire, but the fire of St. Patrick is the new fire of Easter, the new light of Christ.

Two stanzas, the second and the seventh, are directly concerned with the person of Christ. In the second I am reminded of the events of his earthly life, his incarnation, his taking on of human flesh and its redemptive role, and then again in the seventh I am reminded of how that presence is still here now, so that I am totally enclosed and encircled by Christ in the most immediate physical way possible. The sheer physicality of the Celtic tradition is indeed one of its greatest strengths for me. Because the Celtic understanding of the incarnation is deeply physical, fleshly, this then allows me to accept more fully the idea of my own humanity as also so totally physical.

The third stanza takes for granted that we are part of a world of which heavenly beings, spirits, are a natural element. It has become difficult for most of us today to regain a sense of what this would have meant quite unselfconsciously to Celtic peoples, not only in these early times but also until quite recently. "If one does not understand the nearness and apprehensibility of this 'other world' of the angels and the saints, there is no hope at all of understanding Celtic Christianity," says a modern theologian who, brought up in southwest Ireland can speak from his own personal experience.[26]

As I write this, I am sitting at a cottage window in the

Welsh Borders looking across the fields to Graig Syfyrddin (the Hill of the Seraphim) and in any direction that I choose to travel I find evidence in the dedications of small local churches to an awareness of the presence of the angels and the saints, part of the landscape, part of life. The nearness of the invisible world was something entirely natural and so I should not be surprised to find the idea that sun and moon, fire and lightning, wind and ocean, earth and rock, are responsive to the human voice and that as I call upon them they will share with me their strength.

And then in the fifth stanza I am led on to the invocation of the creator. Here are all the powers of the Godhead, and I am given strength so that I am able to face all the enemies and destructive forces that lie in wait for me on the way, some external, some interior. Since I travel under the protection of the Triune God, I can pray for the guarding of body and soul against all perils and dangers. I can call on both nature and grace to come to my aid. Who and what are my enemies? The snares and evil enticements which the lorica goes on to describe make me think of the net into which I fall or the trap that catches me, which the psalmist speaks of time and again. Perhaps it is lies and deceit and, more than anything else, self-delusion, which assail me destructively. When these dark forces threaten me, I know that the sixth stanza rings very true and convincingly.

But now the lorica returns to the figure of Christ and gives me a most lyrical and strong exposition of the presence of Christ in my life. It is only too easy to read the seventh stanza quickly, or pray it casually, with the result that its full significance can become dulled through overfamiliarity. I need to take it phrase by phrase, slowly and contemplatively, entering imaginatively into what it is giving and what it is asking. This stanza makes the indwelling of God a reality for me. But it becomes a *felt* reality only as I reimagine these amazing lines, and actually envisage what they are saying. I have to think of myself as a space, a sacred space, in which God dwells. This can be difficult if I do not value myself very highly or have low self-esteem. Or perhaps I resist the whole idea because I would prefer to keep God distant, safe. Yet here I have to accept that Christ has chosen to live in me already, now. Only as I pray these lines slowly can I take in the fullness of this thought: I am surrounded by Christ in every direction. He is present in every dimension in my life. He is beneath me in the certainty of the ground beneath my feet. He is beside me close at hand, walking with me, on my level, seeing things with the eyes that I see. And so I go on, taking each phrase in turn, and trying to realize the full implication of what I am saying— and praying.

But it is not only personal. As I would expect from anything Celtic, I am always being brought back to a corporate and shared spirituality. I shall see and find Christ in others: in the hearts and tongues and eyes and ears of all whom I meet on my journey. This is the call of St. Benedict to see all who come as Christ. It prevents any inward journey from becoming one of interior self-exploration, and instead tells me that it is one of belonging, of relationships. The key is given in the word "love" that comes at the start and again here at the end, in the first and eighth stanzas. Is my journey that of love? It is the question that St. Benedict asks throughout the Rule: <u>am I becoming a more loving person?</u>[27] It is the question that I once heard an African priest address to us Europeans as he spoke of his own African Christian understanding: <u>Is the journey an inward one that involves growth into relationships</u>? I know that this is the most essential question of all. If I am going to take St. Patrick's breastplate as the protecting prayer for my journey, then I will find that I allow the power of the Trinity into my life: the Godhead of a multiplicity of persons in a unity of love. And so here is a blessing from the *Carmina Gadelica* which asks so simply for the protection of the Trinity on the journey that I am making:

> *The guarding of the God of life be upon me,*
> *The guarding of loving Christ be upon me,*
> *The guarding of the Holy Spirit be upon me,*
>   *Each step of the way,*
> *To aid me and enfold me,*
>   *Each day and night of my life.*[28]

2

IMAGE AND SONG

"WHEN THE IMAGE of the God of life is born into the world, I put three little drops of water on the child's forehead." As Alexander Carmichael traveled through the Highlands and islands of western Scotland at the end of the last century, he not only collected from the local people their poems and songs and prayers and blessings (it is impossible to separate them) but also the stories of the way in which they still kept alive in their households many of the rituals and customs that had been passed down in oral tradition from generation to generation. We have this account in the words of Peggy MacCormack of the birth-baptism, which preceded the clerical baptism, the baptism in church eight days later by the priest:

> I put the first little drop in the name of the Father, and the watching-women say "Amen." I put the second little drop in the name of the Son, and the watching-women say "Amen." I put the third little drop in the name of the Spirit, and the watching-women say "Amen." And I beseech the Holy Three to lave and to bathe the child and to preserve it to Themselves. And the watching-women say "Amen." All the people in the house are raising their voices with the watching-women, giving witness that the child has been commit-

ted to the blessed Trinity. By the Book itself! ear has never heard music more beautiful than the music of the watching-women when they are consecrating the seed of man and committing him to the great God of life.[1]

So at the very start of its life the newborn child was committed to the three persons of the Trinity, and we find the same keynote as with the lorica of asking the protection of the arms of Mary and Christ "shielding and surrounding and succoring the joyous little sleeper of the baptism." But there were other customs as well. "When a child was born it was handed to and fro across the fire three times, some words being addressed in an almost inaudible murmur to the fire-god. It was then carried three times sun-wise round the fire, some words being murmured to the sun-god." So at the same time that the child was being commended to the Trinity it was also being inserted into the world of the primal elements of fire and of water, and its connectedness to the earth itself was established right away as it was carried around the hearth in the direction of the sun's daily movement.

There is in the Celtic oral tradition a whole treasury of poems and blessings to be used throughout life: from birth to death, from dawn to dusk, from season to season. As I discovered them and began to incorporate them into my own praying, I found myself amazed by the richness of these rituals, the images and symbols that they brought me. I was most moved when I read how, at the start of each day, a woman would rise while her household was still asleep in order to lift the peats of the fire which she had banked down the night before. As the first flicker of flame reappears she makes it the occasion of a prayer for herself, her family, the whole world. The miracle of the fire was never taken for granted, not only because of the vital role it played in their lives in bringing both light and heat, but also because it reminded them that they, too, like the fire, needed constant renewal.

> *I will kindle my fire this morning*
> *In the presence of the holy angels of heaven,*
> *In the presence of Ariel of the loveliest form,*
> *In the presence of Uriel of the myriad charms,*
> *Without malice, without jealousy, without envy,*
> *Without fear, without terror of any one under*
>   *the sun,*
> *But the Holy Son of God to shield me.*
>   *Without malice, without jealousy, without envy,*
>   *Without fear, without terror of any one under*
>   *the sun,*
>   *But the Holy Son of God to shield me.*

This first stanza opens the door to the angelic presences, so that the angels fill the little cottage with the Holy Son of God at their center. Then it moves on to the form of a protection prayer so that the start of each day is placed in the presence of God. And here the protection names the enemies, which are the interior forces of the dark—those impulses toward malice, jealousy, envy, and the rest, the weaknesses of the human heart and will. How well I know these thoughts and how destructive they can be, encouraging me to become competitive and comparative, destroying the thoughts of gratitude and thanksgiving which I know only too well are life-giving. Then the second stanza is all about the heart:

God, kindle Thou in my heart within
A flame of love to my neighbour,
To my foe, to my friend, to my kindred all,
To the brave, to the knave, to the thrall,
O Son of the loveliest Mary,
From the lowliest thing that liveth,
To the Name that is highest of all.
    O Son of the loveliest Mary,
    From the lowliest thing that liveth,
    To the Name that is highest of all.[2]

Here the theme of interiority continues, for it is to do with the kindling within the heart of a fire that mirrors and transcends the fire on the hearth. Just as the fire is kindled on the hearth each day, so also there must be the kindling of an inner fire that mirrors this external fire. This fire, or brightness of love, will shine out to all: "to my foe, my friend, my kindred all." But then it goes even further, in a note perhaps unique to Celtic Christianity, for it reaches out to the whole of nature, "the lowliest thing that lives," a love, in other words, for all that lives, nonhuman as well as human, in a total unity of life.

In a sermon that is virtually a prayer, of St. Columbanus, one of the greatest of all Celtic *peregrini,* he also speaks of love as a flame of love to be kindled, nourished, fed, and kept alive: . . . that He may deign so to inspire us with His love, that He may deign so to arouse us from the sleep of idleness, so to kindle with that fire of divine love, that the flame of His love would mount above the stars, and the divine fire would ever burn within me! Would that I had the tinder to foster, feed, and keep alight that fire unceasingly, and nourish that flame, which knows no quenching, and knows all increase.[3]

This prayer, which the Hebridean woman prayed at the lighting of the fire, would have been intoned or crooned in an undertone while the work was being done rhymically for she lifted the peats in threes, in the name of the Trinity. It gives us a glimpse of a way of praying and living that seems to have been entirely natural to the Celtic peoples of Ireland and Scotland up to the end of the last century, kept alive through oral tradition. Here is praying that is not only inseparable from daily life and work but inseparable from song. Time and again Carmichael will speak of the crooning, or intoning, of words sung under the breath as well as out loud. There was no separation of the religious from the secular: "prayers and charms, songs and hymns, tales and music and dancing . . . whatever the people might be doing, or whatever engaged in, there would be a tune of music in their mouth . . ."[4] Children must not only have been deliberately taught them by their parents but they must also have watched, observed, overheard these prayers until they became so interwoven into their lives that quite naturally this became also their own way of praying.

It began, of course, at the very moment of birth. As Carmichael was given this song, he was told how lovely were the words of the womb-woman and how beautiful it was to hear her:

> A small drop of water
>> To thy forehead, beloved,
> Meet for the Father, Son and Spirit,
>> The Triune of power.

> A small drop of water
>> To encompass my beloved,
> Meet for Father, Son and Spirit,
>> The Triune of power.

> A small drop of water
>> To fill thee with each grace,
> Meet for Father, Son and Spirit,
>> The Triune of power.

And then the reciter went on to say how people would be always crowding into one another's houses

> telling tales and histories, invocations and prayers, sing-
> ing hymns and songs, runes and lays . . . the old peo-

ple conversed about the state of the world and about the changes of the weather, about the moon and the sun, about the stars of the sky, about the ebbing and flowing of the sea . . . We children would be sitting on the bare flat of the floor, not uttering a syllable, not moving a hand, lest we should be put out of the house were we not mannerly. O King! 'tis there would be the talk!—and noble talk.[5]

For in this these people were still part of that timeless world that sets store by memory, myth, story, the core that holds all traditional societies together. It has always been the role of the poet to keep this alive. In the Celtic countries poetry was a vehicle for the transmission of what was most important in that society. Who knows the secrets of the world? Not the learned men, but the poets. When a poet joined an early Irish monastery, he had to be taught to cut wood and do manual work since hitherto his art had been with words. The Christian poets, above all the monastic poets, entered into this tradition, and it brought them confidence and status. The importance of "listening to the songs of clear-speaking poets" is a telling line in one early poem. Poetry is the natural teaching medium and the dominant form of public utterance. Indeed in the early Celtic world there was not much concern with prose. "True to their own native tradition they had a marked preference for verse rather than prose as the literary medium most fit for the purpose of praising God and speaking about the mysteries of Christ."[6] Irish monastic rules were written in poetic form and could "even be called poems about the good monks rather than rules in the later sense."[7] The Antiphonary of Bangor, dated circa 680, has not only hymns written in forms new and old, but many prayers intended for daily use which were also in verse, short, rhythmical pieces, generally quatrains, embellished with rhyme and alliteration. There were great numbers of hymns, sung not only either before or after the liturgy but on other occasions in the life of the monastery, for example, at mealtimes, when songs were sung by and for the community as instruction or entertainment. Poetry here fulfills a social function and is not merely the expression of personal feeling. So when we read that St. Columbanus composed many works that were "profitable for instruction or suitable for song," it would seem that in thus equating the two, that song was clearly a natural way in which faith was expressed.

In those earliest years both in Ireland and in Wales the interaction and cross-fertilization of pagan and Christian meant a creative vitality in the response of these countries to Christianity. They were able to adopt the Christian mold without the abandonment or the denial of native culture. As a result, we find the preservation of ancient oral lore and the baptism of the vernacular use as a medium of Christian literature.[8] Already by the sixth and seventh centuries the monastic writers were turning to the native *"filidi,"* poets, when they wanted to put anything down in writing. "By the seventh century the monks had accepted the pagan tradition and put it on one level with the historical material which came down to them under the sanction of the fathers of the church."[9]

How different all this is from the instruction I received

as I grew into my own Christian faith. I was taught to recite the creeds, I was prepared for confirmation on the basis of a catechism that in effect told me that there were certain articles of belief to which I must subscribe. My head was constantly engaged, my mind filled with information. But this did not involve the whole of myself, my five senses, my emotions and feelings, and above all my imagination. Nor did it bring any sense of continuity or belonging, seeing myself as being inserted in my own generation into a great and continuing heritage of the past. I had no sense of being a member of a long chain of family and kin stretching back into the past, and so being able to draw from a shared common storehouse of memory and storytelling. If I am discovering how to pray differently (and also to think and to feel differently), it is because I am now finding a holistic way which better responds to the wholeness and the fullness within my own self. And this of course helps me to become the person who I would much prefer to be.

But above all the Celtic tradition has reminded me of the importance of images, those foundational images whose depths and universal character have always brought such riches to Christian understanding. Most people today are being constantly battered by the succession of superficial images that meet us in the world of consumerism, in television and in advertising, where there is no chance to spend time testing their true meaning. Therefore, it now becomes vital, more than ever, to recover the fundamental images of fire, wind, bread, water, of light and dark, of the heart. These are the great impersonal symbols that are universal, understood by Christian and non-Christian alike. An Indian Christian priest once said that they were like a great bridge that Christ has thrown across the world and across history so that men and women may walk to meet each other and be completed in him.[10]

3

THE TRINITY

ALREADY I AM discovering that the Celtic journey inward is not made alone. Celtic spirituality is corporate spirituality with a deep sense of connectedness to the earth itself and the natural elements, to the human family, not only the present immediate family into which each of us is born, but the extended family as it stretches back in time through the many generations. In today's society, which increasingly likes to treat us as isolated units, and which seems to encourage an individualistic and competitive approach to life, the Celtic tradition brings another set of values. It speaks instead of harmony, unity, interrelationship, interdependence, and all that is meant by coinherence, that word so beloved of Charles Williams, whose deepest meaning has not yet fully unfolded itself for me.

The God whom the Celtic peoples know is above all the Godhead who is Trinity, the God whose very essence is that of a threefold unity of persons, three persons bound in a unity of love. Here is a profound experience of God from a people who are deeply Trinitarian without any philosophical struggle about how that is to be expressed intellectually. Perhaps the legend of St. Patrick stooping down to pick up the shamrock in order to explain the Trinity is after all more significant than we might have thought. It is as though he were saying to those early Irish people: Your God is a God who is Three-in-One and this is the most natural and immediately accessible thing in the world! We saw in the previous chapter how in the Hebrides at the end of the last century the mother immediately committed her newborn child to walk for the rest of its life with the three persons of the Trinity "in friendliness and love." Again it is entirely natural, taking place at home, around the hearth, in the midst of family and neighbors.

This is not a Trinity that is remote, distant, inaccessible. I can remember that when as a child I was asked what my favorite hymn was, I would tell everyone that it was "Immortal, invisible, God only wise, In light inaccessible hid from our eyes." It was partly to impress, but it was also because the God whom I met in church on Sundays and to whom I addressed my daily prayers in the week was indeed a remote authority figure, stern, unknowable. What I have found in the Celtic tradition is utterly different. These people were at ease in speaking of the Trinity, finding analogies not only in nature but also in daily life, as in these traditional lines from Ireland in which the Trinity is spoken of in terms of the greatest simplicity:

> *Three folds of the cloth, yet only one napkin is there,*
> *Three joints in the finger, but still only one finger*
>   *fair*
> *Three leaves of the shamrock, yet no more than one*
>   *shamrock to wear,*
> *Frost, snow-flakes and ice, all in water their origin*
>   *share*

Three Persons in God; to one God alone we make
    prayer.[1]

This holds a close affinity to something written by the seventeenth-century Welsh writer Morgan Llwyd:

> The Trinity abides with us exactly the same as the ore in the earth, or a man in his house, or a child in the womb, or a fire in a stove, or the sea in a well, or as the soul is in the eye, so is the Trinity in the godly.[2]

But then, traditionally the Celtic people with their love of formulating things and their passion for significant numbers have always given special veneration to the number three. Most beloved of all was the triad, an arrangement of three statements that summed up a thing or person or quality or mood, or simply linked otherwise incompatible things. If there were a paradox or a pun in a triad, so much the better, for they were, above all things, paradoxical.[3]

As we have noted, the prayers sung over the child at the birth-baptism in the home have a great simplicity and gentleness. They were repetitive with much of the same quality as a mother rocking a child to and fro in her arms, caressing, reassuring, and above all taking time:

> *The little drop of the Father*
>   *On thy little forehead, beloved one.*

> *The little drop of the Son*
>   *On thy little forehead, beloved one.*

The little drop of the Spirit
    On thy little forehead, beloved one.

To aid thee from the fays,
    To shield thee from the host;

To keep thee from the gnome;
    To shield thee from the spectre;

To keep thee from the Three,
    To shield thee, to surround thee;

To save thee for the Three,
    To fill thee with the graces;

The little drop of the Three
    To lave thee with the graces.[4]

A woman in Barra when reciting her birth-baptism song told Carmichael that she would put three drops of water on the forehead of the "poor little infant, who has come home to us from the bosom of the everlasting father," and then she gave him a prayer that ended with the following three verses:

The little drop of the Three
To fill thee with Their pleasantness.

The little drop of the Three
To fill thee with Their virtue

O the little drop of the Three
To fill thee with Their virtue.[5]

The Trinity is now indwelling in the child and each member brings a different blessing and has a differing role to play. The mother whispers quietly into the ear of her newborn, telling the child what is its birthright:

The blessing of the Holy Three little love, be dower
*   to thee,*
Wisdom, Peace and Purity.

This blessing gives to each member of the Trinity their own peculiar, particular attribute:

I send witness to Father,
*   Who formed all flesh;*
I send witness to Christ,
*   Who suffered scorn and pain;*

I send witness to Spirit,
*   Who will heal my wound,*
Who will make me as white
*   As the cotton-grass of the moor.*[6]

This invocation opens by calling on the saints for the help that each can give according to their own stories. Thus St. Brigit is the tender nurse of the Lamb, St. Michael is the noble warrior triumphant, St. Columba is the apostle of shore and sea, and St. Peter, so very humanly, is apostle of fear and of sleep.

Another prayer, collected by Douglas Hyde at the same time in Ireland, is very brief and to the point:

> O Father who sought me
> O Son who bought me
> O Holy Spirit who taught me.[7]

So I take up these ideas and try to make them a part of my own praying journey. I think of the making and creating role of the Father, and how much in my life can be seen as cooperation with that: anything that I do to create, to awaken, to cherish new life; what I do to mold and shape the environment, such as the clearing of the tangle of briars and undergrowth strangling the new life in a neglected corner of the garden, my manual work to keep the hedges clear of throttling brambles as well as the more profound creating of new human flesh in my own womb and the cherishing of that in my children's early years. Now, in more recent years, there has been the creating and making with words, to be shaped and handled and used with delight and care, as well as the more mundane but equally satisfying work in the kitchen of making meals and washing the dishes. To the Son who bought my freedom I commend all that I may try to do in working with people, teaching and listening, trying to expand inner horizons, trying to widen hearts and imaginations through the sharing with others of what I have myself received from my study of St. Benedict or Thomas Merton, the Cistercian Fathers or the Celtic tradition. Finally to the special role of the Holy Spirit I commend all the work of compassion and forgiveness and healing that must happen time and again throughout my life, the mending and making whole again, and how my own receiving of the gifts of compassion and acceptance and forgiveness can then be shared.

But it is always to the Three-as-One that prayer is made—prayer which sees the Godhead in its cosmic context:

> The Three Who are over me,
> The Three Who are below me,
> The Three Who are above me here,
> The Three Who are above me yonder,
> The Three Who are in the earth,
> The Three Who are in the air,
> The Three Who are in heaven,
>   The Three Who are in the great pouring sea.[8]

The Eastern idea of Christ as the head and center of the created world was well preached when Christianity was first introduced into Ireland, and there is much in the early monastic writings, above all in that great hymn of the monks of Bangor the *Hymnus Dicat* written between 680 and 691 which speaks of Christ's kingship as the center of life in the Trinity.[9] There are many hymns and celebrations of creation that link creation with the Trinity. Perhaps the greatest of all is the *Altus Prosator* of St. Columba, a great hymn of praise and in the words of Manus O'Donnell, the sixteenth-century biographer of St. Columba "a composition

passing lofty and passing noble, but passing hard of understanding: for therein he giveth from his knowledge of the
secrets he had from God. And in especial he speaketh much
of the meaning of the Trinity . . ."[10] The opening verse is
a most splendid manifestation of the Trinitarian emphasis
that shapes what is to follow:

> *The High Creator, the Unbegotten Ancient of Days,*
> *was without origin of beginning, limitless,*
> *He is and He will be for endless ages of ages,*
> *with whom is the only-begotten Christ, and the*
> * Holy Spirit,*
> *co-eternal in the everlasting glory of divinity.*
> *We do not confess three gods, but say one God,*
> *saving our faith in three most glorious Persons.*[11]

This is a great declamatory statement of belief, a credal
confession of faith, a declaration of orthodox doctrine and
at the same time a most glorious piece of writing. I do not
want to treat it as I did the creeds that shaped my early
upbringing, when I stood stiffly as though it were for the
National Anthem, shoulder to shoulder with my mother
and my sister in the vicarage pew as we all made this public
statement weekly about our faith. I want to be able to take
my Trinitarian understanding into my daily life, into my
praying and living, and words such as this help me to do
that. I want to be able to stay with these words, meditate on
them, let them wrap themselves around my heart as well as
my intellect. In the *Life of St. Ide* there is a nice moment
when she is asked how it is that she was able to do what she

did, and she replies, quoting her questioner, "You yourself have answered your question when you said: 'You continue daily without interruption in prayer and in meditation on the Holy Trinity.' If anyone acts thus God will always be with him, and if I have been so from childhood, therefore all those things happened to me."[12]

Blathmac was a sixth-century monastic poet who rewrote the biblical account of creation and redemption in a long poem full of images so vivid and original that he has caused me to stop and look at things anew. He addresses the poem to Mary, and here he is telling her about her son who, as a member of the Trinity, is the creator of the world:

> *Your son Christ, it is clear, is one of the three*
> *persons of the deity, and all things, indeed, have*
> *been created by him.*

> *He is in union with the Father, with the Holy Spirit;*
> *he is their peer; it is from Them, with the permission*
> *of all, that the Holy Spirit proceeds.*

The verses in which he describes Christ as the overlord of the world which he has created bring me infinite delight:

> *This is my clear announcement: your son is king of*
> *the heavens. His the brightly clothed sun, his the*
> *gleaming moon.*

*His is the earth to his will; it is he who moves the
sea; both has he endowed, the one with plants and
the other with sea-creatures.*

*He is the most generous that exists; he is a
hospitaller in possessions; his is every flock that he
sees, his the wild beasts and the tame.*

*Your son of fair fame owns every bird that spreads
wings; on wood, on land, on clear pool, it is he who
gives them joy.*[13]

When I pick up the *Carmina Gadelica* or the *Religious Songs
of Connacht* I find that the Trinity is naturally a part of the
daily labor-songs or the seasonal work-songs. The day starts
with three palmfuls of water splashed on the face in the
name of the three members of the Trinity, and from then
on the Trinity is never far away. The day will end with the
ritual of smooring the fire at night, a ceremony which the
woman told Carmichael was "artistic and symbolic, and is
performed with loving care." The embers were spread
evenly on the hearth in the middle of the floor and formed
into a circle with a small boss, or raised heap, left in the
middle. This circle was then divided into three equal sec-
tions with a peat laid between each section, each peat
touching the boss, which was called the Hearth of the Three
which formed the common center. The first peat was laid
down in the name of the God of Life, the second the God of
Peace, and the third the God of Grace. The circle would
then be covered over with ashes sufficient to subdue but not

extinguish the flame in the name of the Three of Light.
Then the woman would close her eyes, stretch out her hand,
and softly intone the following prayer, which opens:

> *The sacred Three*
> *To save,*
> *To shield,*
> *To surround*
> *The hearth,*
> *The house,*
> *The household,*
> *This eve,*
> *This night,*
> *Oh! this eve,*
> *This night,*
> *And every night,*
> *Each single night.*
> *Amen.*[14]

This Trinitarian emphasis lends itself particularly well to
any work that was done rhythmically. There is an example
of this in the making of cloth when it reached the stage of
the waulking. It was placed on a frame in order to be thick-
ened and brightened, and the waulking-women would be
ranged on either side of the frame and they sang as they
worked. Toward the end of the process it was the custom for
it to be consecrated (the woman who led the consecration
being called the consecrator or celebrant), in which they
named each member of the household for whom it was
intended. The women would sing in unison while the cloth

was spat upon and slowly reversed end by end in the name of the Father, the Son, and the Spirit.[15]

A late twelfth-century poem on the Trinity is much more formal and conventional than either the early monastic writings or the household songs of the oral tradition.

Teach me, O Trinity
All men sing praise to Thee,
Let me not backward be,
Teach me, O Trinity.

Come Thou and dwell with me,
Lord of the holy race;
Make here Thy resting-place,
Hear me, O Trinity.

That I Thy love may prove,
Teach Thou my heart and hand,
Ever at Thy command
Swiftly to move.

Like to a rotting tree,
Is this vile heart of me;
Let me Thy healing see,
Help me, O Trinity.[16]

This, though it lacks much of the simplicity and freshness of most of the work quoted in this chapter, still has one most lovely phrase, "Make here Thy resting-place." That says it all. It is this deep sense of relationship within the three persons of the Trinity, and the relatedness of that to my own self, which the Celtic Trinitarian understanding has given me. It allows me to be at ease with a mystery that no longer threatens but supports, refreshes, and strengthens me.

4

TIME

THERE IS ONE image that has helped me to appreciate the Celtic understanding of time, and to enter more fully into the sense of the pattern, flow, and rhythm of time in one's life, and that is the Irish bell tower. It is a unique Celtic artifact and, after a recent visit to Ireland, I can still picture those I saw vividly. Many are dramatically tall, with a delicate conical cap, as at Glendalough, rising high above the ruins of the monastery, the lakes, and the hills. Some are ruined, neglected, one I found ivy-covered, inhabited by flocks of rooks, but still keeping guard over the broken walls of a monastic church and a worn, high cross. One was no more than a broken base in the middle of a field. And then in contrast there are those that continue to dominate a busy market town, as at Kildare, or Kells or Kilkenny. They had meant much as I stood touching their stones, gazing in admiration at their amazing elegent beauty, but above all grateful for what they said about the Celtic sense of the presence of God. Much has been written about building technique and dating and style, but in the end when scholars come to answer questions about the purpose of the towers, they simply say: "As to why these towers were built there is ultimately only one answer. They were raised to the greater glory of God as symbols reaching up towards heaven to mark in unmistakable fashion the strongholds of the new faith."[1]

These towers are found only in Celtic countries, mostly in Ireland, two in Scotland, and one on the Isle of Man. They are slender and beautiful—and significant. They stand tall, rising to a hundred feet or more, dominating the surrounding landscape, a point of reference for many miles around. They are always associated with a monastic community and, although later on they may serve a useful purpose in becoming towers of refuge in the times of Viking raids, in origin they were what their name in Irish *cloigtheach* says—a house for the bell. That bell was not, of course, the bell as we know it today, with a rope, hung in the tower of the parish church, but a metal bell, iron or bronze, without a clapper, which would be struck not rung. An early poem calls it "the throbbing bell," and speaks of the reverberant boom of the bell, of its metal voice.[2] At the top there are four windows opening to the four points of the compass and from that great height the sound of the bell would reach for miles across the surrounding countryside. People hearing it would know that it was a call to prayer, reminding them that as they were at work in farm or household, their local monastic community was interrupting its own working life for the *opus Dei*, "the work of God," the saying of the daily round of prayer that marked their days. So the message that the towers gave, and still bring today if we are prepared to see them as an image, is that the pattern of each day is punctuated by the call to prayer (much as in Muslim countries the sound is rung out from the minaret). Life must flow into prayer, each day is to be broken up by times of prayer, praying and living are inseparable.

Early Celtic Christianity was above all monastic. People learned their religious beliefs and practices from the monastic communities with the monastic ideal of continual prayer. The spirituality of ordinary lay people was a monastic spirituality; ordinary lay people expected to pray the daily offices, which means, of course, essentially to follow a liturgical life shaped by a regular, ordered rhythm—yearly, seasonal, daily. It reminds us of that sense of rhythm which today's world seems to be losing. Life today for many people is life under constant pressure, and even for those who are not in the business world there is still so often a sense of things needing to be done, and to be done to meet a deadline. Yet in monastic living there is a seasonal, yearly liturgical pattern that recognizes the importance both of regularity, and of the breaking of that regularity by celebration, by rest days, by festivals. Here is something that is natural, healing, and sanctifying. The chief moments of the day are marked through the seven offices: the quiet of the night, dawn, the beginning of work, noon, sunset, and at the end compline, the completion of the day. And then the yearly calendar recognizes the changing pattern of each year, marrying the winter and the spring seasons to the church's festivals. Today when I can go into a supermarket and buy any of the fruits of the earth at any time of the year I need no longer be aware of the pattern of the earth bringing forth her fruits in due season. Living with electricity, I can deny the night and I can extend the day entirely to suit my own self, my needs, and my interests. I can forget the coming of the dark or the slow dawning of the light; the pattern of the rising and the setting of the sun, or the waxing and waning of the moon, are no longer really important.

The liturgical pattern of the monastic daily offices creates a life that is "structured, disciplined, repetitive, supremely orderly." A modern psalter widely used in Cistercian monasteries today speaks of "the strict and exquisite order of the liturgical day, of the Christian year," and these are words which I find express what I have found, both the strength and the delicacy of this framework of prayer.[3] To lose this is a great impoverishment, for it denies the balance that a holistic way of life brings—due recognition given to the needs of body, mind, and spirit, so that we find time for work, for study to keep the mind alive, but above all proper time for prayer. Without this I know that I would probably become either exhausted, or lethargic, unhealthy, diseased.

But a sense of rhythm also has a wider significance for the Celtic peoples in that it kept alive awareness of the relationship, the interplay between the light and the dark, both daily and yearly. The Celtic year begins with the feast of Samhaine on November 1, the time when in the northern hemisphere men and women began to think of the coming of winter, of the dark. It is the thinnest time of the year, the season at which the veil between time and eternity can easily become transparent, the time when darkness overtakes the light. It is still, in the parlance of country people, "the turning of the year, the passing of the year." If I try to imagine what life would have been like in the fifth and sixth centuries, when Christianity was first introduced to these completely rural people, close to the earth and to the pattern of the year, I think what waiting for the coming of winter must have meant: the season that would bring suffering and possible death to many. November, the first month of winter, was in fact known as the dark or the black month in Scotland, Cornwall, and Brittany. It was a time quite literally for drawing in, when the flocks were brought down from the summer pastures to be wintered at the homestead. The bonfires we associate with early November are in fact the bone-fires, the burning of the inedible parts of the carcasses of animals that could not be kept throughout the winter. But then the year swings forward to the summer festival, the feast of Beltaine on May 1, when the flocks are taken back to the upper pastures, and there the promise of summer, of light, of long days and short nights. The dancing at the maypole is a reminder of this annual celebration, and of the two points that divided the year in half. The place names found in the Welsh landscape, *hendre* and *hafod,* the winter and the summer homesteads, recall this timeless annual movement of people and animals (as does *shieling* in Scotland, the place of summer pasture).

Early Celtic Christianity accepted all of this and handed it over to God. The Christian year took this pattern which spoke of an annual movement from darkness and fear to light and warmth. So time consists of the alternation of opposites: light and dark, warmth and cold, life and death. This is a Christian faith and experience that has never been fearful of taking up and of Christianizing what it found in the existing religion—and in doing so it has thereby touched something that is early, primal in human understanding and the way in which traditional people naturally live their lives.

In much of the earliest Celtic nature poetry there is a strong sense of the contrast of the seasons. Here is an expression of what midwinter means:

In the dark seasons of deep winter
heavy seas are lifted up
along the side of the world's region.
Sorrowful are the birds of every meadow-field,
except the ravens of dark-red blood,
at the uproar of fierce winter-time.[4]

And here is another, late ninth- or early tenth-century Irish, written on May Day:

May Day, season surpassing!
Splendid is colour then.
Blackbirds sing a full lay,
If there be a slender shaft of day.

The dust-coloured cuckoo calls aloud:
Welcome, splendid summer!
The bitter bad weather is past,
The boughs of the wood are a thicket.

Summer cuts the river down
The swift herd of horses seeks the pool,
The long hair of the heather is outspread,
The soft white wild-cotton blows.

Panic startles the heart of the deer,
The smooth sea runs apace,
Season when ocean sinks asleep
Blossom covers the world . . .

Delightful is the season's splendour
Rough winter has gone,
White is every fruitful wood,
A joyous peace is summer.

A wild longing is on to you race horses
The ranked host is ranged around;
A bright shaft has been short into the land,
So that the water-flag is gold beneath it.[5]

And that penultimate line, of course, is speaking of a sun-beam, or the ray of the summer sun.

This pattern of the seasons, as of the day itself, depends on the sun. We should not forget the place that the sun has always held in early worship. We still know little of the meaning of the very earliest stone megaliths, but we know of their association with the sun, and that it was the solar movement that almost certainly dictated their positions. The lesser divisions of the year are a reflection of the movement of the sun. The four cross-quarter days that come between the equinox and the solstice divide the year into eight parts, the lesser seasons of the agricultural year. They have also become Christian festivals: the winter solstice the feast of St. Thomas, the summer solstice the nativity of John the Baptist, the spring solstice Lady Day on March 25, and Michaelmas in the autumn.

The Celtic tradition, therefore, reminds us to honor the sun as a gift from a God who is the God of light and fire and warmth. Beltaine was the feast of "the sun's fire." The modern Irish term for dawn is literally "the ring of light on the sky-line at day-break." A monastic tradition in which "the loving-kindness of the heart of our God, who visits us like the dawn from on high," words from the Benedictus sung at the start of each day, is speaking a language that would seem natural to a people who honor the dawn, and who rejoice in the sun's rising and setting. Alexander Carmichael found that in the Outer Isles old men would still uncover their heads when they first saw the sun as they came out of the house each morning. He says that they would hum a hymn that was "not easily caught up and not easily got from them":

> *The eye of the great God,*
> *The eye of the God of glory,*
> *The eye of the King of hosts,*
> *The eye of the King of the living,*
>> *Pouring upon us*
>>> *At each time and season,*
>> *Pouring upon us*
>>> *Gently and generously.*

>> *Glory to thee,*
>>> *Thou glorious sun.*

Glory to thee, thou sun,
Face of the God of life.[6]

There was another sun custom and a prayer that he recorded from an old man in Arasaig. "When the sun would rise on the tops of the peaks he would put off his head-covering, and he would bow down his head, giving glory to the great God of life for the glory of the sun and for the goodness of its light to the children of men and to the animals of the world. When the sun set in the western ocean the old man would again take off his head-covering, and he would bow his head to the ground and say:

> " 'I am in hope, in its proper time,
> *That the great and gracious God*
> *Will not put out for me the light of grace*
> *Even as thou dost leave me this night.' "*[7]

The old man told Carmichael that he had learned this from his father and from the old men of the village when he was a small child. This gives us a glimpse of the role of the men in keeping alive the pattern of prayer, and reminds us that it was not just the women of the family who would help the children to pray.

If the people saluted the morning sun, they also hailed the new moon. They hailed the morning sun as they would a great person come back to their land; and they hailed the new moon, "the great lamp of grace," with joyous welcome and acclaim. The sun was to them a matter of great awe, but the moon was a friend of great love who guided them along the path at night, whether by land or by sea. For a seafaring people the light and guidance of the moon was a matter of much importance, often indeed a matter of life and death. On a moonless night they could only thread their way through tortuous rocks and reefs and channels in great danger of death. So both sun and moon had their gifts and played their roles, something that was never forgotten: "I think myself that it is a matter for thankfulness, the golden-bright sun of virtues giving us warmth and light by day, and the white moon of the seasons giving us guidance and leading by night."[8]

I learn much from a people who never cease to celebrate the sun and the moon, together with the stars, "that the great God of life made for my good" as an old man from Barra put it.[9] There were still many rituals which Alexander Carmichael found associated with the first sight of the new moon, turning a coin three times in the pocket being one of the most common, or making the cross of Christ upon the palm of the hand with spittle. Men and women might go to the highest hill or knoll near them to watch for its appearance, and there was competition as to who should see the new moon first. This praising ritual was not one solely for humans, for the creatures were included as well. Herdboys and herdgirls might whisper softly in the ear of the cow, "There is the new moon, thou beloved one among cows."

> When I see the new moon,
>   It becomes me to say my rune;

It becomes me to praise the Being of life
   For His kindness and His goodness![10]

Or again,

   I am lifting to thee my hands,
      I am bowing to thee my head,
   I am giving thee my love,
      Thou glorious jewel of all the ages.

   I am raising to thee mine eye,
      I am bending to thee my head,
   I am offering thee my love,
      Thou new moon of all the ages![11]

A people who farmed and knew the pattern of the seasons, who lived close to the sea and watched the ebb and flow of tides, above all who watched the daily cycle of the sun and the changing path of the moon, brought all of this into their prayer. Here is a way of praying that is essentially holistic. I am reminded that as a human being living on this earth I am a part of the pattern of day and night, darkness and light, the waxing and waning of the moon, the rising and setting of the sun. The whole of my self is inserted into the rhythm of the elements and I can here learn something, if I am prepared to, of the ebb and flow of time and of life itself.

   The holding together of dark and light, cold and warmth, came naturally to a people whose whole livelihood showed death and rebirth, dying and new life, was a natural and inevitable part of their existence. Only those who know nothing of nature can be entirely romantic about living close to the soil. Creation comes with pain. The furrowing of the earth, the sowing of the seed, the time of waiting, the uncertainty until the ripening of the harvest, is a demanding way of life. But a succession of rituals upheld and sacramentalized it. There were, for example, many ceremonies, songs, and prayers used each year at seedtime and at harvest. Three days before it was sown, the seed was sprinkled with clear, cold water in the name of Father, Son, and Spirit, the person who was doing the sprinkling walking sunwise with great care and solemnity. This moistening had the effect of hastening its growth when it was finally sown, generally on a Friday, the most auspicious day for sowing— which may have had some pre-Christian element but in its Christian context refers to Friday as the day of Christ's death and burial, and Christ who is King of Friday is the seed of the new world of the resurrection of men and women and of nature.

The theologian Noel Dermott O'Donoghue can look back on a childhood growing up in southwest Ireland, where, for every step of the work, for each of the successive seasons of the year, there was a ritual, an appropriate prayer. He can appreciate the significance of what he was then experiencing quite unconsciously when he was a young boy, and as he writes about the farmer sowing the seed he allows us to see something of the quality of that life:

The seedsman is his own priest. The work is equally labor and liturgy . . . He is exactly situated in space and time in a world where each little field, each hillock and valley, has a name, and where not only each of the four seasons is noted but many lesser seasons as well, each with its own character and related to man's independence.[12]

Here is the long prayer that Carmichael found being used in Scotland.

I will go out to sow the seed,
In name of Him who gave it growth;
I will place my front in the wind,
And throw a gracious handful on high.
Should a grain fall on a bare rock,
It shall have no soil in which to grow;
As much as falls into the earth,
The dew will make to be full.

Friday, day auspicious,
The dew will come down to welcome
Every seed that lay in sleep
Since the coming of cold without mercy;
Every seed will take root in the earth,
As the King of the elements desired,
The braird will come forth with the dew,
It will inhale life from the soft wind.

I will come round with my step,
I will go rightways with the sun,
In the name of Ariel and the angels nine,

In the name of Gabriel and the Apostles kind.
Father, Son and Spirit Holy,
Be giving growth and kindly substance
To every thing that is in my ground,
Till the day of gladness shall come.

The Feast Day of Michael, day beneficent,
I will put my sickle round about
The root of my corn as was wont;
I will lift the first cut quickly,
I will put it three turns round
My head, saying my rune the while,
My back to the airt of the north;
My face to the fair sun of power.[13]

The day on which reaping began was no less a day of ceremony. The whole family went to the field dressed in their
best attire to hail the God of the harvest. Laying his bonnet
on the ground, the father of the family took up his sickle
and, facing the sun, would cut a handful of corn. Putting
this three times, sunwise, around his head, he raised the
reaping salutation, and the whole family took up the strain
and praised the God of the harvest who gave them "corn
and bread, food and flocks, wool and clothing, health and
strength, and peace and plenty."

God, bless Thou thyself my reaping,
Each ridge, and plain, and field.
Each sickle curved, shapely, hard
> *Each ear and handful in the sheaf.*[14]

Each day of the week also carried its own importance. Sowing had to be done on a Friday, but any work that involved the use of iron might not be done on a Friday—for the memory of the use of iron nails on the cross was not forgotten, and a blacksmith would never open his smithy on a Friday. "That was the least he could do to honour his Master" he told Carmichael.[15] Thursday was St. Columba's day, and was looked upon as a lucky day for many enterprises: for warping thread, for the marking of lambs, and many other undertakings.

> *Thursday of Columba benign,*
> *Day to send sheep of prosperity,*
> *Day to send cow on calf,*
> *Day to put the web in the warp.*
>
> *Day to put coracle on the brine,*
> *Day to place the staff to the flag,*
> *Day to bear, day to die,*
> *Day to hunt the heights.*
>
> *Day to put horses in harness,*
> *Day to send herds to pasture,*
> *Day to make prayer efficacious,*
> *Day of my beloved, the Thursday,*
>   *Day of my beloved, the Thursday.*[16]

Sunday was, of course, a day of rest. When Carmichael took down this poem from a woman in South Uist, he remarked that poems similar to this might be traced back to the eighth century, and the fact that he could seriously claim this seems to me an important indication of the amazing continuity of this Celtic heritage, carried down by lay people from generation to generation in their household settings.

The poem of the Lord's Day, O bright God.
Truth under the strength of Christ always.

On the Lord's Day, Mary was born,
Mother of Christ of golden yellow hair,
On the Lord's Day Christ was born
    As an honor to man . . .

The Lord's Day, the seventh day,
God ordained to take rest,
To keep the life everlasting,
Without taking use of ox or man,
Or of creature as Mary desired,
Without spinning thread of silk or of satin,
Without sowing, without harrowing, without reaping,
Without rowing, without games, without fishing,
Without going to the hunting hill,
Without trimming arrows on the Lord's Day,
Without cleaning byre, without threshing corn,
Without kiln, without mill on the Lord's Day.
Whosoever would keep the Lord's Day,
Even would it be to him and lasting,
From setting of sun on Saturday
Till rising of sun on Monday.[17]

Beltaine remained the central festival in the cycle of the agricultural pastoral year, the season of light, the time of growth. It was then that the sheep and cattle would be driven up to the summer pastures, the "shielings" in Scotland, the "hafods" in Wales. This was a virtual migration since these might be six or eight or even twelve or fourteen miles away, and it often meant crossing land that was rough and rugged or full of swamps, even sometimes having to swim across channels or rivers. The procession included the men carrying spades, ropes, and other things that might be needed to repair their summer huts, while the women carried the bedding, meal, and dairy utensils. As they went, there were songs to be sung on the journey, a dedicatory hymn to the Trinity and to the most familiar of the saints, Michael, Bride, and Columba, respectively the protector, the woman who knew about dairies, the guardian of their cattle—and, of course, to Mary herself, who on this occasion they address as mother of the White Lamb:

> *Valiant Michael of the white steeds,*
> *Who subdued the Dragon of blood,*
> *For love of God, for pains of Mary's Son,*
> *Spread thy wing over us, shield us all,*
> > *Spread thy wing over us, shield us all.*

> *Mary beloved! Mother of the White Lamb,*
> *Shield, oh shield us, pure Virgin of nobleness,*
> *And Bride the beauteous, shepherdess of the flocks*
> *Safeguard thou our cattle, surround us together,*
> > *Safeguard thou our cattle, surround us together.*

And Columba, beneficent, benign,
In name of Father, and of Son, and of Spirit Holy,
Through the Three-in-One, through the Trinity,
Encompass thou ourselves, shield our procession,
    Encompass thou ourselves, shield our procession.

O Father! O Son! O Spirit Holy!
Be the Triune with us day and night,
On the machair plain or on the mountain ridge
Be the Triune with us and His arm around our
    head,
      Be the Triune with us and His arm around
      our head.[18]

Because this comes from a distant place, a rural world, which seems to naturally have an inbuilt sense of pattern and order, there is a very real danger that we might either patronize it by seeing it as romantic and escapist, or dismiss it as irrelevant to the way in which we live in the twentieth century. What underlies it is something that I want to re-cover for a more holistic way of living and praying: the link between men and women and the earth; the daily pattern of the coming of light and the fall of darkness; the movement of the seasons of the year; the relationship of death and new life and rebirth, time and time again.

5

THE PRESENCE
OF GOD

AT THE HEART of what I have been writing about in the previous chapter is a deep sense of the presence of God—God here and now, with me, close at hand, a God present in life and in work, immediate and accessible. It is not merely that I learn this as some sort of abstract theory, something that I can repeat as a statement of faith—it is given to me in terms that are practical, usable, in a whole treasury of poems and prayers and blessings that I can take over and use in my daily life, from the opening of the day until I fall asleep at night. Both the early monastics of those very earliest centuries in the Celtic Church and the men and women whom I have come to know from their words, collected at the end of the last century by Douglas Hyde and Alexander Carmichael, have this in common: they were a people who were at home in themselves, in the place in which they found themselves. A monastic vocation comes out of stability in the deepest meaning of that word: for many of the Celtic monks and nuns were, of course, *peregrini,* wanderers who moved from one community to another, often from one country to another. But they did not try to escape from themselves or from God. Ironically many of the farmers and crofters of the nineteenth century probably knew a great deal more actual geographical stability than the monks, born and dying in one particular place, working the land, familiar with each small hill and field that lay around them. From both I learn what is commitment, and how that means simply staying still, not trying to escape, being deeply rooted in one's innermost self.

From this center (the place that ironically I guess they knew better than many of us do today in spite of all the help available to us in the techniques and technologies of self-knowledge!) there comes this vivid sense of a God who knows, loves, supports, is close at hand, and actually present in their lives. Of course this sense of divine presence and protection are found elsewhere in the history of the Church, but I feel that nowhere else is it found with quite the same intensity. It is one of the many gifts of the Celtic tradition to us, and it is perhaps the most important. "The Gaelic race see the hand of God in every place, in every time and in every thing," wrote Hyde.[1] "They have this sense of life being embraced on all sides by God." They speak of God dwelling in his world, and in our lives in such a way that Emmanuel, God with us, becomes a reality. It is there right from the start in St. Patrick's breastplate, with its "Christ within me," the indwelling God, who is claimed in a way that is virtually tangible. This is a God physically present, alongside, behind, before, above, below. God is companion, guest, fellow traveler, friend, fellow worker. Some of the most-used words that we find in these prayers are *encircle, encompass, uphold, surround.* This flows from their real, lived-out grasp of the centrality of the incarnation. "God with us" is true! Of course they also know God as transcendent, and they write quite superbly of God as the creator God, all-powerful, all-knowing. But they also know that he is present here and now in the world that he has made.

These are simple prayers, but we should not be misled by that. They come out of hearts that are full of gratitude, thankfulness. They are not beseeching God to give them this, or grant them that. They are recognizing that God has showered them with blessings and they thank him for what he has given. This is, of course, very much in the Hebrew tradition, to bless God, who has done this and who has given that, to bless him for his gifting of us. They are generous prayers, not claiming all these good things for ourselves alone but wishing to share them. So they bring us back to two aspects of prayer that we might easily neglect. They remind us of gratitude. They remind us of a shared and corporate spirituality.

In this they have much in common with prayers of other traditional peoples, such as this from the Iroquois, for whom blessings were thanks for what is already there:

Our religion is all about thanking the Creator.
That's what we do when we pray.
We don't ask Him for things.
We thank Him.
We thank Him for the world and every animal and
    plant in it.

We thank Him for everything that exists.
We don't take it for granted that a tree's just there.

We thank the Creator for that tree.
If we don't thank Him maybe the Creator will take
  that tree away.

That's what the ceremonies are all about—that's why
they are important—even for the White Man
We pray for the harmony of the whole world.
The Creator wants to be thanked . . .[2]

"Prayer should be cast wide" is a traditional Irish saying. These prayers are never self-engrossed, they open up circle after circle, always moving outward. They come out of a sense of family, extended family, household. This should hardly surprise us since in its earliest origins the Celtic tradition was shaped in a people for whom kin and kinship were of paramount importance, together with a monasticism where the emphasis is on loving relationships within the community.

In the prayers that Douglas Hyde and Alexander Carmichael collected, we find an oral tradition, which is essentially a lay spirituality. Praying is not associated with going to church. Praying and living were not set apart, distinct. Dominic Daly, who had come to know the Irish tradition well, has this to say about them:

They came from a people for whom active living faith was a positive factor of daily life. There is nothing posed or formal about them. For the men and women who recited them prayer was not a formal exercise: it was a state of mind. Life was lived under the shadow of

God's outstretched arm. His protection was constantly sought. His aid and help was constantly sought. . . . They have in them something of the breadth and depth of the psalms. Awe and dread of the might of God and of His anger at sin is more than balanced by trust in his love and mercy.[3]

The collection that Douglas Hyde made is less well known than that of Alexander Carmichael, and so in this chapter I shall be drawing on that whenever I can.[4] As he traveled he found that in every quarter of Ireland there were a great number of short petitions or prayers in the form of poetry, which had come down from past ages. It was quite impossible, he said, to separate charms, blessings, poems, prayers, curses—these things are all mixed together in this book.[5] They were all part of the living faith that was such a vital part of their lives, and must surely account for the fact that Carmichael found that people could give "account of the faith that was in them."[6] Prayer was not separate from poetry and from song. These were people who were singing all the time, from the start of the day until its end. Prayers were keened or crooned or sung under the breath—they were not said silently. This would have had an incalculable effect on children, who from the start of their lives must have been aware of parents praying, would watch and hear prayer as a natural part of daily life. They would also, of course, find that the words became familiar to them. When Carmichael tells us, almost in passing, that this ended as people became *talkative*, he is saying something the significance of which we should not miss. The way of life that we are being shown here is one that is essentially <u>contemplative</u>. Here are ordinary lay people like myself living extremely busy lives, and yet prayer is the undercurrent of whatever they are doing. It was entirely unselfconscious, of course, and that was part of its strength. Here is a life full of dance and celebration and not at all pious or solemn, a life lived close to God just as it was close to neighbors and to the natural world. It is this totality that speaks to me, and which I see as one of the most important gifts of the Celtic on my journey into prayer.

The regularity of this prayer was one of its strengths. As regular as the saying of the daily monastic office were prayers from the moment that anyone awoke, which covered all the most mundane and inevitable chores: washing, making the bed, starting the fire, milking, making butter, weaving, and so on throughout the day. Since this way of life, without machinery or electricity, is now remote for most of us, there is a very real danger that we could romanticize it. We should not forget that for much of the time it must have been hard, dull, heavy, and boring. And yet I believe that it was fulfilling, for the basic attitude was that of taking matter and the material world, and thus the incarnation, seriously.

Everything that they touched, every tool that they handled, was done with respect and reverence; every activity performed with a sense of the presence of God, indeed done in partnership with him. So life was lived at two levels. Each successive task performed seriously, carefully, with attention, and simultaneously becoming the occasion for finding the presence of God, and in particular the three members of the Trinity, since much of the work was routine and it could, therefore, be done rhythmically in the name of Father, Son, and Holy Spirit. "These are the prayers of a people who have so much to do from dawn to dusk from dark to dark," says Eleanor Hull, another writer who knew the Irish well, "that they had little time for long, formal prayers. Instead throughout the day they make each activity in turn the occasion for prayer, doing what has to be done carefully for its own sake but simultaneously making it into the occasion for prayer. Each thing in turn, however humble, however mundane, can be handed over to God, or performed in partnership with the cooperation of the Trinity, saints and angels."[7] What Douglas Hyde saw in the Irish was a people for whom God was "a thing assured, true, intelligible. They feel invisible powers before them, and by their side, and at their back, throughout the day and throughout the night."[8]

The sense of the three persons of the Trinity is particularly strong, for each can be acclaimed and asked for help in appropriate fashion, as we saw in the second chapter. From the moment of its birth the child was committed to the Trinity in "friendliness and love," and this sets the pattern for the rest of its life. This was recalled daily in this rune before prayer, a hymn sung to start the day:

> I am bending my knee
> In the eye of the Father who created me,
> In the eye of the Son who purchased me,
> In the eye of the Spirit who cleansed me,
>   In friendship and affection.[9]

Here is another that promises the presence and protection of the Trinity:

> *God with me lying down,*
> *God with me rising up,*
> *God with me in each ray of light,*
> *Nor I a ray of joy without Him,*
> > *Nor one ray without Him.*
>
> *Christ with me sleeping,*
> *Christ with me waking,*
> *Christ with me watching,*
> *Every day and night,*
> > *Every day and night.*
>
> *God with me protecting,*
> *The Lord with me directing,*
> *The Spirit with me strengthening,*
> *For ever and for evermore,*
> > *Ever and evermore, Amen.*
> > *Chief of Chiefs, Amen.*[10]

The prayer at rising which follows asks for God's blessing on the day in its wholeness and ends with a reference to the Trinity in a most lovely small phrase "The Three that seek my heart."

> *Bless to me, O God,*
> > *Each thing mine eye sees;*
> *Bless to me, O God,*

> *Each sound mine ear hears;*
> *Bless to me, O God,*
> > *Each odour that goes to my nostrils;*
> *Bless to me, O God,*
> > *Each taste that goes to my lips;*
> > *Each note that goes to my song,*
> > *Each ray that guides my way,*
> > *Each thing I pursue,*
> > *Each lure that tempts my will,*
> > *The zeal that seeks my living soul,*
> *The Three that seek my heart,*
> > *The zeal that seeks my living soul,*
> *The Three that seek my heart.*[11]

As they dressed, children were encouraged by their mothers not to be slow in putting on their clothes and to "clothe our souls with grace while clothing our bodies with raiment."

> *Even as I clothe my body with wool*
> *Cover Thou my soul with the shadow of Thy wing.*[12]

When they washed their faces, it was done carefully, each palmful of water thrown in the name of the Trinity.

> *The palmful of the God of Life,*
> *The palmful of the Christ of Love,*
> *The palmful of the Spirit of Peace,*
> > *Triune*
> > *Of grace.*[13]

Making the bed again provided them with the opportunity to reflect on God's many blessings—and reading this I ask myself if I have ever thought of daily thanking God for the occasion of my conception? The words come from a man in Ireland, Peter O'Corcoran in Inismeadhon:

> *I make this bed*
> *In the name of the Father, the Son and the Holy*
> *   Spirit*
> *In the name of the night we were conceived,*
> *In the name of the night we were born,*
> *In the name of the day we were baptised,*
> *In the name of each night, each day,*
> *Each angel that is in the heavens.*[14]

I have earlier looked at the prayers for the lifting of the peats and the kindling of the fire (see p. 30), and there are numerous prayers such as this, both from Scotland and Ireland, which mark the start of each new day. They all make it clear that this is a ritual of recovery and rebuilding, the renewal of a fire that really never dies, taking all the symbolism there that relates both to the hearth and to the human person.

One of the pleasures in using these prayers is that we come to know the names of many who otherwise would be forgotten, the ordinary men and women whose personal prayers these were. I find myself able to pay homage to other women, humble, busy, ordinary women for whom their faith was a living force and who transmitted that to their children—and as a result to us today. Catherine Maclennan was a crofter who was taught by her mother, who in turn had heard this from her own mother "as she again heard it from the one who was before her." These were women who were always at work, helping the men on the croft by day and at night spinning clothes for the family. "My mother would be beseeching us to be careful in everything," she told Carmichael. She ensured that the day started for her children in a state of mindfulness which I find most moving. Again we see this awareness of the unity of the universe, which goes back to the very earliest beginnings of Celtic Christianity, expressed with great simplicity.

> My mother would be asking us to sing our morning song to God down in the back-house, as Mary's lark was singing it up in the clouds, and as Christ's mavis was singing it yonder in the tree, giving glory to the God of the creatures for the repose of the night, for the light of the day, and for the joy of life. She would tell us that every creature on the earth below and in the ocean beneath and in the air above was giving glory to the great God of the creatures and the worlds, of the virtues and the blessings, and would *we* be dumb![15]

In this short morning prayer there is an emphasis on the wholeness of things, which begins with the unity within one's own self:

> *Bless to me, O God,*
>   *My soul and my body;*

Bless to me, O God,
  My belief and my condition;

Bless to me, O God,
  My heart and my speech,
And bless to me, O God,
  The handling of my hand;

  Strength and busyness of morning,
Habit and temper of modesty,
Force and wisdom of thought,
And Thine own path, O God of virtues,
  Till I go to sleep this night;

  Thine own path, O God of virtues,
  Till I go to sleep this night.[16]

The blessing of the hands means that throughout the day whatever is handled is handled with an awareness of the presence of God. It could hardly be more specific than in this milking prayer that speaks of the partnership with God and asks a blessing on each teat and each finger:

Bless, O God, my little cow,
  Bless, O God, my desire;
Bless Thou my partnership
  And the milking of my hands, O God.

Bless, O God, each teat,
  Bless, O God, each finger;
Bless Thou each drop
  That goes into my pitcher, O God![17]

Some of the prayers must have been very ancient, as this which calls on the sun and the moon, and Douglas Hyde, who collected it, had to confess that he had no idea who the "Men" might be!

The blessing of Mary, and the blessing of God,
The blessing of the Sun, and the Moon in her road,
Of the Man in the East, and the Man in the West,
And my blessing be with thee, and be thou blest.[18]

St. Brigit was naturally someone of whom women were very aware as they worked in the dairy and the kitchen. According to tradition, when she was making butter she had divided the churning into twelve in honor of the apostles, and the thirteenth portion, in honor of Christ, was greater than the others and to be given to the poor and guests. As she did her task, this was her song:

Oh, my Prince
Who canst do all these things,
Bless O God—a cry unforbidden—
My kitchen with Thy right hand!

My kitchen,
The kitchen of the white God,
A kitchen which my King hath blessed,
A kitchen that hath butter.

Mary's Son, my Friend cometh
To bless my kitchen.[19]

In an Irish prayer for churning, St. Brigit's aid is sought because the woman sees the disciples standing outside her house waiting for her to finish so that they can enjoy her butter on her baking. She works with the idea of doing her best, not for the reasons that we so often work hard for today: to excel, to compete, to show our own competence. Here work is done well because it is a sharing of gifts, not only for the poor but also for Jesus himself, his mother, and the apostles:

Come, thou Calum Cille kindly,
   Hasten the lustre on the cream;
Seest thou the orphans unregarded
      Waiting the blessing of the milk-wave
         of the kine.

Come, thou Brigit, handmaid calm,
   Hasten the butter on the cream;
Seest thou impatient Peter yonder
      Waiting the buttered bannock white and yellow.

Come, thou Mary Mother mild,
   Hasten the butter on the cream;
Seest thou Paul and John and Jesus
   Waiting the gracious butter yonder.[20]

Noel Dermott O'Donoghue can recall in his childhood growing up in southwest Ireland what happened when anyone visited a house when they were in the middle of churning. On entering they would give the greeting that was never omitted by a visitor where work was in progress, "Bail o Dhia"—"God's blessing on the work." They would then take the churn staff in their hand and strike the cream with it a number of times, helping it to break copiously into good butter. This extraordinarily simple but significant act of transforming cream into butter carried a lot of meaning: it was a sharing in the work and in the community created by the work, but it was more than this, it was also the involvement of men and women in the very process of creation.

Many of the graces before meals make reference to the feeding of the five thousand, the multiplication of the loaves and fishes, so that the theme is still that of the sharing of blessings. "The good of the five loaves and of the two fishes as God divided them on the five thousand men. Luck from the King who made the division, on our share and on our co-division."[21] Variants of this prayer, we are told, are to be found in Ireland in places as far apart as Meath and Mayo, Donegal and Waterford, which suggests a common origin.[22] This grace is an expression of a hospitality which is ready to welcome all and share with all:

Bless O Lord the food we are about to eat,
and we pray you O God may it be good for our body
  and our soul
and if there is any poor creature hungry or thirsty
  walking the road
may God send him in to us so that we can share the
  good
    with him—just as He shares his gifts with all
      of us.

Here is another which is extremely simple:

Great Giver of the open hand,
We stand to thank Thee for our meat,
A hundred praises, Christ, 'tis meet.
For all we drink, for all we eat.[23]

After the preparation of food, the making of cloth probably would occupy the greater part of a woman's time within the house. When she stopped weaving on Saturday night, she carefully tied up the loom and suspended a cross above it to keep away all evil spirits or malign influences from disarranging the thread and the loom. The prayer is again totally specific. There is no idea that God would be affronted by the mention of different parts of the machine, or that technical terms might be inappropriate to introduce into prayer, and so she lists the thrums, pedals, cogs, and warp. This tells me something about my own way of praying—that it should not be polite, sanitized. If she, my unknown mentor, should find it natural to ask a blessing on the sleay and on the shuttle, then I might ask a blessing on this computer at which I am now at work, on its screen and the keys, the software, the hardware, the flow of the electric current.

Bless, O Chief of generous chiefs,
My loom and everything a-near me,
Bless me in my every action,
Make Thou me safe while I live.

From every brownie and fairy woman,
From every evil wish and sorrow,
Help me, O Thou helping Being,
As long as I shall be in the land of the living.

In name of Mary, mild of deeds,
In name of Columba, just and potent,
Consecrate the four posts of my loom,
Till I begin on Monday.

Her pedals, her sleay, and her shuttle,
Her reeds, her warp, and her cogs,
Her cloth-beam, and her thread-beam,
Thrums and the thread of the plies.

Every web, black, white, and fair,
Roan, dun, checked, and red,
Give Thy blessing everywhere,
On every shuttle passing under the thread.

Thus will loom be unharmed,
Till I shall arise on Monday;
Beauteous Mary will give me of her love,
And there shall be no obstruction I shall not
  overcome.[24]

When the web of the cloth had been woven, it would be waulked. This was an operation to thicken and strengthen it, by which the web was placed on a waulking frame raised on trestles, with the women ranged on either side, about two feet of space being allowed to each woman. The women soaked it with ammonia and worked it vigorously from side to side, and as they slowly turned it, they made sure that it was always sunwise. When this was done, they rolled up the web and placed it in the center of the frame, again turning it slowly and deliberately sunwise. Then came the consecration of the cloth by three celebrants who moved the cloth in turn. The first would say, "I give a turn sunwise," and then complete the circle with the words "dependent on the Father." The following two women turned the web similarly in the name of Son and in name of Spirit, and then the three would finally sing together:

And each sunwise turn
  Dependent on the Three.[25]

Each member of the household for whom the cloth was intended was mentioned by name in this consecration:

This is not cloth for priest or cleric,
But it is cloth for my own little Donald of love,
For my companion beloved, for John of joy,
And for Muriel of loveliest hue.[26]

As I read about this, I see women's work that is shared work and leads naturally into shared prayer. I see an attention to detail in which each element is commended to God, each woof and warp, and each individual person for whom the cloth is intended—the entire process consecrated to God, as that final act shows. Everything takes place with such a vivid and immediate sense of God's presence that he is actually assumed to be a participant in the action to the extent of placing his arm around each woman as she waulks.

Place Thou thine arm around
Each woman who shall be waulking it,
And do Thou aid her in the hour
   Of her need.[27]

The men also have left us the prayers they used in their daily work. For many, life was pastoral, and we know the prayers they used as they took their flocks to the pastures or looked after them on the hills. Customs might vary with different agricultural districts, but they all shared the simple belief that the King of the shepherds watched over men and flocks today just as he did of old. When a man had taken his herds to the pastures in the morning, he would bid them a tender farewell on leaving them, and, waving both hands toward them, would chant or intone what Carmichael calls a patriarchal benediction:

> *The keeping of God and the Lord on you,*
> *The keeping of Christ always on you,*
> *The keeping of Carmac and of Columba on you,*
> *The keeping of Cairbre on you going and coming*
> *And the keeping of Ariel the gold-bright on you,*
> > *The keeping of Ariel the gold-bright on you.*
> *The keeping of Bride the foster-mother on you,*
> *The keeping of Mary the yellow-haired on you,*
> *Of Christ Jesus, the Son of peace,*
> *The King of kings, land and sea,*
> *And the peace-giving Spirit, everlasting, be yours,*
> > *The peace-giving Spirit, everlasting, be yours.*[28]

All these prayers have the sense that God, the saints, and the angels are walking alongside men and women and that it is quite natural to turn to them for support and companionship not only for themselves but also for the animals in their care—which is why I love so much the phrase that comes in this prayer "the friendship of God the Son" for his cattle:

> *Pastures smooth, long, and spreading,*
> *Grassy meads aneath your feet,*
> *The friendship of God the Son to bring you home*
> *To the field of the fountains,*
> > *Field of the fountains.*

Closed be every pit to you,
Smoothed be every knoll to you,
Cosy every exposure to you,
Beside the cold mountains,
  Beside the cold mountains.

The care of Peter and of Paul,
The care of James and of John,
The care of Bride fair and of Mary Virgin,
To meet you and to tend you,
  Oh! the care of all the band
  To protect you and to strengthen you.[29]

Sea prayers and hymns were common among those who lived close to the sea, and Carmichael thought that some of these might go back to the earliest days of Celtic Christianity, when the monks were constantly crossing the seas in their frail coracles and praying for protection from the elements. He knew of many small oratories, simple structures looking out to sea, around the west coast of Scotland, where men would go to pray before and after their voyages. Here God is addressed in terms appropriate to the needs of an oceangoing people:

Be Thou with us, O Chief of chiefs,
Be Thou Thyself to us a compass-chart,
Be Thine hand on the helm of our rudder,
Thine own hand, Thou God of the elements,
Early and late as is becoming,
  Early and late as is becoming.

Just as with the women's prayers, there is no hesitation in being totally specific, both as to people and things:

> Bless our boatmen and our boat,
> Bless our anchors and our oars,
> Each stay and halyard and traveller . . .[30]

Much time was spent in journeys, whether on land or sea, and any journey, long or short, can become a walk with God. A cottar, Dugall MacAulay, told Carmichael that he always crooned this little hymn to himself when he was leaving his house and that he always derived comfort from it:

> God, bless to me this day,
>   God, bless to me this night;
> Bless, O bless, Thou God of grace,
>   Each day and hour of my life;
> Bless, O bless, Thou God of grace,
>   Each day and hour of my life.
>
> God, bless the pathway on which I go,
> God, bless the earth that is beneath my sole;
>   Bless, O God, and give to me Thy love,
> O God of gods, bless my rest and my repose;
>   Bless, O God, and give to me Thy love,
> And bless, O God of gods, my repose.[31]

This same man gave to Carmichael another of the prayers that he would always recite under his breath whenever he

set out on any journey, however short the distance, or however small the matter of his errand. I love it for the way in
which those opening two lines speak of the earth itself, of
the human person and the relationship with the earth, and
finally the way in which it ends up with the eye, which
speaks to me of the vision, the attitude, the way we see the
world:

> *Bless to me, O God,*
>> *The earth beneath my foot,*
> *Bless to me, O God,*
>> *The path whereon I go;*
> *Bless to me, O God,*
>> *The thing of my desire;*
>>> *Thou Evermore of evermore,*
> *Bless Thou to me my rest.*
>
> *Bless to me the thing*
>> *Whereon is set my mind,*
> *Bless to me the thing*
>> *Whereon is set my love;*
> *Bless to me the thing*
>> *Whereon is set my hope;*
>>> *O Thou King of kings*
> *Bless Thou to me mine eye!*[32]

The strength of these prayers, and their importance for me,
is that just like the prayers of the monastic life itself, they
are said with regularity. There is certainty about each daily
activity being accompanied by prayer. Just as for the monas-

tics there was prayer at rising and they ended their day with
the saying of Compline, so also for these lay people the day
began and ended with prayer. The smooring of the fire
meant that the fire was banked down at night so that it
would be found alive again the following morning (see
pp. 47–48 for the ritual involved). This prayer, which, according to Hyde, was "to be found in every place in Ireland
and in Scotland also" could be said:

As I save this fire tonight
Even so may Christ save me,
On the top of the house let Mary
Let Bride in its middle be,
Let eight of the mightiest angels
Round the throne of the Trinity
Protect this house and its people
Till the dawn of the day shall be.[33]

Another smooring prayer from Ireland has a nice variant:

"Mar smuairim an tenine seo—"
As I rake the ashes over this fire,
They are raked by the Son of Mary.
Blessed be house and fire!
Blessed be the people under this roof!
Let an angel stand at the great door,
Until the ring of day shows in the East.[34]

As a result, at nightfall they go to bed with the certainty of
the presence of God, who has been with them throughout

the day and who is perhaps even closer in the hours of darkness. There are a great many bed blessings and they are among the most delightful of all these Celtic prayers. It was difficult for them to think of sleep without death, and impossible to think of either without God, the saints and the angels, and Mary herself, being there beside them. There is peculiar tenderness in these prayers, for God is always addressed with great familiarity and love. Carmichael said that when at the end of each day they spoke these last prayers, their language was "so homely yet so eloquent, so simple yet so dignified" as they spoke to "the great God of life, the Father of all living."[35]

I am lying down to-night as beseems
In the fellowship of Christ, Son of the Virgin golden,
In the fellowship of the gracious Father of glory,
In the fellowship of the Spirit of powerful aid.

I am lying down to-night with God,
And God to-night will lie down with me,
I will not lie down to-night with sin, nor shall
Sin or sin's shadow lie down with me.

I am lying down to-night with the Holy Spirit,
And the Holy Spirit this night will lie down with me,
I will lie down this night with the Three of my love,
And the Three of my love will lie down with me.[36]

6

THE SOLITARY

ON THE TOP panel of many Irish high crosses there is a scene which when I first saw it immediately caught my imagination, and has continued to do so ever since. It shows two hermits, St. Antony of Egypt and St. Paul of Thebes, meeting together in the Egyptian desert. Above their heads is a raven, for the story tells that every day a raven brought St. Paul half a loaf of bread, but on the day that St. Antony was to visit him brought him a whole loaf. So there they stand, these two old men, a bird hovering above their heads, breaking and sharing bread in the wilderness—and the fact that the bread is so often shown in the shape of a round loaf makes the Eucharistic implications even more apparent. It is because these two solitaries come from the hermit tradition that they are so important to me. Many of these crosses were put up at the height of the Céile Dé movement in the eighth century, when monasticism was reclaiming its er-emetical emphasis, an emphasis that had in fact been there right from the start. If I now consider the hermit tradition and its implications for my own journey of prayer, it is because it is an essential element in Celtic Christianity just as it is an inescapable element in my own life.

Here is a spirituality shaped and formed by those men and women of the Egyptian desert who wanted to escape the Church as it was developing after the time of Constantine, frightened by what they saw of its growing wealth and property and prestige. They left the cities and fled into the desert in order to find there what they believed was at the heart of the Christian life: time for prayer, silence and solitude, externally and internally, with sufficient manual work to earn their living. The essential concern was to stay in one's cell, to enter into the cave of the heart. "A certain brother went to Abbot Moses in Scete, and asked him for a good word. And then the elder said to him: 'Go, sit in your cell, and your cell will teach you everything.' "[1] Here is something essential, inescapable for any of us. Unless we learn to live with ourselves, how can we live with others? Unless we know ourselves, accept ourselves with honesty and forgiveness, how can we possibly know or accept other people? I know that maturity comes only from staying still, from facing what has to be faced, perhaps from engaging in a battle with the forces that threaten me from within and without. Yet in all my years of growing up, no one, neither my own family, my school, or college, helped me to think about what was involved in living with myself. In my more adult years I have not found a church that has taught me this, and it is only in recent years that I have begun to find books and retreats that have given me some practical help and experience and wisdom.

In Wales and in Ireland there are still as many as five hundred place names, *disserth* or *dysart,* that recall the claiming of this desert of the heart. Here in the landscape is testimony to their way of life, that of the Egyptian desert under totally different physical circumstances. There is one not so far from where I live, and I find it strangely moving to visit it and to see where, in a small valley, beside a stream in what would then have been deeply wooded country, a hermit would have lived in the sixth century. Often sites were on remote stretches of coast or on islands, such as the island of Bardsey off the Llyn peninsula in North Wales. Bardsey is still today sufficiently remote (without electricity or telephone, and likely to be cut off in bad weather) for it to be possible to experience something of what it would have been like for those early hermits.

By the destiny of their vocation to silence and solitude, these early Celtic hermits found themselves living in places of extraordinary beauty. They allow us to see it through their eyes, since they have left us some of the most amazing nature poetry. It is nature poetry with a difference. They saw the world through eyes washed miraculously clear by continual spiritual exercise; they saw with "rinsed eyes" . . .[2] They saw with such clarity because the seeing came out of their contemplative vision. And their writing reflects this, with its distinctive freshness and immediacy, its attention to detail. This is not descriptive verse that sometimes tends to become shallow, superficial, sentimental. Neither is it primitive or romantic. But it is imaginative, vitally felt and expressed with emotional insight so that it can still today produce a shock of delight in the reader.[3] There is a particular sensitivity toward color that reminds me of the variety and subtlety of the *Book of Kells.* For whereas in a Greek lyric or in Anglo-Saxon poetry there are adjectives that mean "bright" or "flashing" or "pale," and so on, Celtic literature uses constantly distinctive color words, often going into minor varieties of a color, such as "red, rusty-red, blood-red, sky-blue, grayish-brown"—"the dust-colored cuckoo calls aloud," "the peat-bog is as the raven's coat." It is as if each poet were rediscovering the world for himself so that a moment will be caught with amazing clarity, as in a crystal ball, never petrified.[4]

Monastic life of whatever culture or tradition knows about awareness, mindfulness, a total listening to God, living in the present, being alive to the world around, finding in that world the visible a reflection of the invisible. This is, of course, also true of the way in which the poet sees the world, so when the two come together in one person it is hardly surprising to find that we have such extraordinary poetry.

Irish nature poetry is the earliest and freshest in any vernacular, very different from classical Greek or Latin lyrics. Nature is seen with the natural eye, in specific detail, described with an economy of detail, a concentration on the simple, the essential, the vivid. There are no long elaborate or drawn-out ideas. Rather, there is a very special beauty, a grave and strong simplicity. Here are a few verses from a long tenth-century poem:

Smooth the tresses   of yew-tree, yew-trees,
   glorious portent;
place delicious   with great green
   increasing blessing.   oakwoods

Tree of apples,   huge and magic,
   great its graces;

crop in fistfulls   from clustered hazel,
  green and branching.

Sparkling wells   and water-torrents,
  best for drinking;
green privet there   and bird-cherry
  and yew-berries.[5]

Here is the mind in tune with the heart. The lightness and the joyousness of the phrases can still startle today. They have the sure touch of the Japanese haiku, or the sure brush of the Impressionist painter. By never saying too much, but instead leaving much unsaid or half said, they allow us in some mysterious way to identify with their experience. Here is something that is universal. When I read some Celtic nature poems to a gathering of Japanese poets in Tokyo, they found that they felt immediately at home.

I have a hut in a wood: only my Lord knows it, an ash tree closes it on one side, and a hazel like a great tree by a rath on the other.

The size of my hut, small, not too small, a homestead with familiar paths. From its gable a she-bird sings a sweet song in her thrush's cloak.

A tree of apples of great bounty like a mansion, stout: a pretty bush, thick as a fist, of small hazel-nuts, branching and green.

Fair white birds come, herons, seagulls, the sea sings
to them, no mournful music: brown grouse from the
russet heather.

The sound of the wind against a branching wood,
grey cloud, riverfalls, the cry of the swan, delightful
music!

Beautiful are the pines which make music for me
unhindered: through Christ I am not worse off at
any time than you.

Though you relish that which you enjoy exceeding all
wealth, I am content with that which is given me by
my gentle Christ.

With no moment of strife, no din of combat such as
disturbs you, thankful to the Prince who gives every
good to me in my hut.[6]

As the poets enter into harmony with nature, that brings a
closer unity with God. They see themselves as part of the
whole created world, related to it in a unitive simplicity,
well expressed in a tenth-century poem attributed to St.
Manchan:

I wish, O Son of the living God,
eternal, ancient King,
for a secret hut in the wilderness
that it may be my dwelling.

A very blue shallow well
to be beside it,
a clear pool for washing away sins
through the grace of the Holy Ghost.

A beautiful wood close by
around it on every side
for the nurture of many-voiced birds
to shelter and hide it.

Facing the south for warmth
a little stream across its ground,
a choice plot with abundant bounties
which would be good for every plant . . .

This is the housekeeping I would get,
I would choose it without concealing,
fragrant fresh leeks, hens,
salmon, trout, bees.

My fill of clothing and food
from the King of good fame,
and for me to be sitting for a time
praying to God in every place.[7]

This is not thinking about the world at one remove, not
using nature as "a scenic backdrop for the poet's own psychological state or a metaphor for the human condition."[8]
This helps me to stop *thinking* about the world and instead

to start feeling and seeing with something of this same immediacy. Sometimes I walk slowly and carefully, making it an exercise in awareness, often with a magnifying glass so that as I pick up tiny leaves, a scrap of lichen, a rock, and spend time looking intently, I find secret and hidden patterns I could never otherwise have begun to imagine. As I do this I begin to see something of underlying unity in the shape of the things I handle. And then seeing and praying and praising flow together into one whole.

These hermits wrote out of their overwhelming sense of the goodness and graciousness and generosity of a God who showers abundant blessings on his creation for which the only response can be to praise him. But they also remember what George McLeod called in a vivid phrase "the dry lichen of sins long dead." So while there is constant praise, above all in the daily saying of the psalms, in concert with the singing of the birds and the sound of the wind in the trees or the lap of the waves on the shore, they also never forget the need for repentance.

This simple rule of an eighth-century solitary presents the toughness of the hermit life without any illusion:

All alone in my little hut without any human being in my company, dear has been the pilgrimage before going to meet death.

A remote hidden little cabin, for forgiveness of my sins; a conscience upright and spotless before Heaven.

Making holy the body with good habits, treading it boldly down; feeble tearful eyes for forgiveness of my passions.

Eager wailings to cloudy Heaven, sincere and truly devout confession, fervent showers of tears.

A cold anxious bed, like the lying-down of the doomed, a brief apprehensive sleep, cries frequent and early.

My food to suit my condition—it is a dear bondage—my meal would not make me full-blooded, without doubt.

Dry bread weighed out, well we bow the head; water of the fair-coloured hillside, that is the draught I would drink.

Stepping along the paths of the gospel, singing psalms every hour: an end of talking and long stories: constant bending of the knee.

My Creator to frequent me, my Lord, my King, my spirit to seek him in the eternal kingdom where He is.

This is the end of vice among mansions, a lovely little cell among many graves, and I alone there.

*All alone in my little hut, all alone so, alone I came
into the world, alone I shall go from it.*

*If of my own I have done wrong at all, through the
pride of this world, hear my wail for it all alone, O
God!⁹*

There are many things in this poem that I love, but especially the glimpse that we are given in that phrase toward
the end of the storytelling that must have been such a fea-
ture of contemporary life, and has now given place to listening to the Gospel and singing the Psalms.

The hermit life must often have been harsh and un-
lovely, cells dark and damp, nature threatening as often as
she smiled. No easy paradise here! Nature is often cruel:

*Grey branches have wounded me,
they have torn my hands;
the briars have not left
the making of a girdle for my feet.¹⁰*

By entering the cell, the cave of the heart, we encounter God
and we encounter our own selves. In the totality of that
encounter there is dark as well as light, dark forces that are
as frightening, destructive, menacing, throttling as the wind
and storm, or the briars and brambles outside. At
Glendalough St. Kevin looked out over a lake whose traditional name was "the lake of the monster," and he chose a
cell on the side of the lake where for six months of the year
the sun did not shine so that he actually put himself into

the shadow. When Seamus Heaney, the Irish poet, visited one of the small hermit oratories on the west coast of Ireland, he found in the building itself an image of the hermit life. "Inside, in the dark of the stone, it feels as if you are sustaining a great pressure, bowing down like generations of monks who must have bowed down in meditation and reparation on that stone cold floor." Here he felt you knew:

> the weight of Christianity in all its rebuking aspects, its calls to self-denial and self-abnegation, the humbling of the proud flesh and insolent spirit. But coming out of the cold heart of the stone into the sunlight and dazzled of grass and sea, I felt a lift in my heart, a surge toward happiness that must have been experienced over and over again by those monks as they crossed that same threshold centuries ago.[11]

> *Cells that freeze,*
> *The thin pale monks upon their knees,*
> *Bodies worn with rites austere,*
> *The falling tear—Heaven's King loves these.[12]*

There is no escape from tears! The hermit in his or her cell still carries hurts, fractures, pain, and darkness, his or her own as well as those of the world seemingly left behind. The hermit life speaks of something that is true for us all, which the monastic life has always known, the relationship of microcosm and macrocosm, inner and outer, mirroring each other. Hard things have to be faced. Nor is it a once-and-for-all battle; the briars grow again each year, I clear an open space, a breathing space, but it has to be reclaimed time after time. The weeds that cling, the briars that attack, become reminders of the sins, weakness, failings against which I have all the time to be on my guard—and in the following chapter I shall be looking at how well the Celtic tradition understands the dark forces and how we should approach them. So naturally there are prayers for protection, like this ninth-century hymn attributed to St. Sanctan:

> May Christ save us from every bloody death
> from fire, from raging sea . . .
> may the Lord, each hour come to me
> against wind, against swift waters.[13]

On a recent visit to Skellig Michael on a stormy day in a small boat I could understand only too well the terror of the ocean and its unpredictable forces, and the frailty of the human craft, both literally and metaphorically. With every sense alert to the thrust and power of the wind and waves seemingly coming in all directions, I could glimpse something of the dedication and determination of those hermits to reach their destination. But then I remembered that each day would begin for them with the saying of the Venite, Psalm 95, in which God is acclaimed as "the rock of our salvation." If they were living lives shaped by the daily saying of the Psalms, would it not be natural to find places in which the imagery of the Psalms became an actual part of their lives? The Egyptian desert, after all, would have been a constant reminder of the landscape in which the people of Israel spent their years in the wilderness. So here, in the

West, were men and women drawn to places that helped to bring greater reality to the words that were a part of their daily lives? To say the Psalms on Bardsey or on Skellig Michael forces one to think of the many layers of meaning that the image of rock can bring to prayer—or to the meaning of "under the shadow of thy wing" as the sea birds swoop overhead, or the glorious significance of "the dawn from on high has visited us" at the moment of watching the sun coming over the horizon.

For if there was one certainty, one continuum, in the hermit life, it was the rhythm of the saying of the daily offices, the reading of the Bible, and the saying or singing of the Psalms. The liturgy echoes the changing pattern of the hermit's life, the coming of dawn, the coming of dusk, the drawing in of the year, the lengthening of the days, the planting and the reaping, the arrival of the migrating birds and their disappearance again. Both the regular saying of the Psalms and the regular flow of the seasons in the northern hemisphere would have encircled these hermits. For me the best expression of this is found in some lines of a prayer attributed to St. Columba. As he sits on a headland at Iona and looks across the sea to Ireland which he so deeply loves and from which he is forever exiled, he feels that he is watching a whole revolving feast, of heaven and earth, ebb and flow, angels and humans of which he himself is a part:

Delightful I think it to be in the bosom of an isle, on the peak of a rock, that I might often see there the calm of the sea.

*That I might see its heavy waves over the glittering
ocean, as they chant a melody to their father on
their eternal course.*

*That I might see its smooth strand of clear
headlands, no gloomy thing; that I might hear the
voice of the wondrous birds, a joyful course.*

*That I might hear the sound of the shallow waves
against the rocks; that I might hear the cry by the
graveyard, the noise of the sea.*

*That I might see its splendid flocks of birds over the
full-watered ocean; that I might see its mighty
whales, greatest of wonders.*

*That I might see its ebb and flood-tide in their flow;
that this may be my name, a secret I tell. "He who
turned his back on Ireland."*

*That I might bless the Lord who has power over all,
Heaven with its pure host of angels, earth, ebb,
flood-tide.*[14]

Despite the harshness and severity of their lives, they knew
with utter certainty that this was where they wanted to be.
Perhaps one of the most familiar of all the hermit poems is
that which takes the form of a colloquy between two brothers, one the warrior king, the other the brother who has

renounced the court, its colors, and its festivities for the simple garment of undyed wool and the austerity of a hut in the wood. It opens with the king asking

> *Why, hermit Marvan, sleepest thou not*
> *Upon a feather quilt?*

This is, of course, no more than a literary device for the long reply that follows, an apologia for the hermit life that speaks of the deep contentment that that brings. Even though it might seem to be a life of renunciation, it was in fact a life of fulfillment:

> *Beautiful are the pines which make music for me*
> *unhindered: through Christ I am no worse off at any*
> *time than you.*

> *Though you relish that which you enjoy exceeding all*
> *wealth, I am content with that which is given me by*
> *my gentle Christ.*

> *With no moment of strife, no din of combat such as*
> *disturbs you, thankful to the Prince who gives every*
> *good to me in my hut.*[15]

There was wisdom in that balance of the original Egyptian desert hermit life that recognized that manual labor must always be part of each day, even if the work itself was no more demanding than the weaving of baskets. For the Desert Fathers and Mothers knew, as did St. Benedict, that manual work was not merely a desirable but an absolutely necessary part of their spirituality. For the Celtic hermits there was always the land to be looked after, fish to be caught, fruits gathered, simple physical work with the ability of earthing one, and preventing the very real danger that being on one's own might make one a prey to a world of daydreams, longings, fantasies.

"Care for and study in your hearts what causes the strengthening of your city, that is, pray to God diligently and love him in your hearts, for it is that which causes its strengthening through the help of God, and this then is your strength and the help of God to you."[16] The interior city of the heart has to be known and nurtured. Perhaps it is significant that this quotation comes from a gloss written on Psalm 48:13, for it was above all the regularity of the saying of the Psalms that shaped, fed, and reassured the hermit.

Living the solitary life brings a lesson about the importance of structure, the framework, and orderliness that are vital in order to prevent solitude from breaking down into lassitude, untidiness, lethargy, depression. Each person living on his or her own discovers the cost of not running away, of staying still without giving up, of being totally present to God, one's own self and the place itself—which is stability, a way of living with truth. It is only too easy to speak longingly of the solitary life, of the beauty of silence and solitude (and I notice with a mixture of alarm and amusement the growing popularity of writing about solitude today) without facing its harsh reality.

But we cannot fully appreciate the Celtic hermits without taking into account the part that the birds and animals played in their lives. The stories of their friendships with the wild creatures around them make delightful reading, as anyone who has discovered the translations of Helen Waddell's *Beasts and Saints* will well know.[17] But they are also significant for what they are telling us about the way in which the monastic life, ideally, is a living out of the new creation. Writing from his own hermitage in March 1967, Thomas Merton spoke about this in a letter to Rosemary Radford Reuther:

> I am in the line of the paradise tradition in monastic thought, which is also part and parcel of the desert tradition, and is also eschatological, because the monk here and now is supposed to be living the life of the new creation in which the right relation to all the rest of God's creatures is fully restored. Hence, Desert Father stories about tame lions and all that jazz.[18]

Merton is referring, of course, in his typically laid-back fashion to the story of the friendship of St. Gerasimos (often confused with St. Jerome), who, when he saw a lion hobbling with pain because of a bit of reed stuck in its paw, healed it and brought him back to the monastery. Then there developed such a friendship between them that when St. Gerasimos died, the lion laid itself down weeping on his grave and died too.[19] The saints often performed valuable services to creatures in need, and the animals and birds owed much to their loving care and protection. The story of St. Melangell has become increasingly well known in recent

years as more and more pilgrims come to visit her restored shrine at the place of her hermitage in a secret, hidden valley in mid-Wales. She was a young Irish woman who left Ireland in the sixth century for a life of prayer and solitude in a solitary valley in the Berwyns. There, as she was at prayer one day, the local prince came hunting, following a hare which he saw take shelter under her robes. When he urged on his dogs they withdrew in fright, and when his huntsman lifted his horn to his lips his hands and his horn stuck fast. Seeing this, the prince spoke with Melangell and as a result promised her not only land in the valley but also that the hares would always find protection there.[20]

But the good deeds were mutual. The creatures gave practical help right from the start in finding the site, hauling logs and building the cell before they then settled down to perform useful daily tasks for the hermit. An otter brought St. Kevin a salmon from the lake, a cock woke Mo Chua in time for matins, and a fly walked along every line he read in the Psalter so that if he stopped reading he would not lose the place (see pp. 175–76 for more details). There were also the more spectacular services, such as when the otter rescued St. Kevin's precious Psalter when it had fallen into the lake. Once again we are drawn back to the place that the Psalms play in the hermit's life, and the involvement of the animals with that life of prayer and praise. Stories of ascetic saints being trustfully approached by wild animals and birds and thereafter living in friendship with them are to be found from Syria and Egypt to Ireland, Wales, and Northumbria. They are recounted not merely as wonders but for what they tell us of the intention of these

men and women to imitate on earth the ceaseless praise of the angels, to win back the intimacy with God and the harmony with other creatures that Adam had lost, and to rebuild a harmony that had been broken.[21]

There is one story that draws together all that we have been exploring here. It is that of St. Cuthbert, praying at night in the icy waters of the North Sea. It is a familiar scene through its frequent retelling, and a most charming one when, as he comes up out of the water cold and frozen, two otters appear and lick his feet, wiping them with their skins and warming them with their breath. But if we are to understand this aright, Sr. Benedicta Ward tells us we must do as Bede did, and place over it the lens of the Scriptures. That hidden observer, the brother who is spying on St. Cuthbert in this hour of his most secret prayer, is not seeing a man alone by the sea with two small furry animals rubbing round his ankles, he is watching the epiphany of God by water and by light, a moment of vision:

> He had not been watching a man on a beach with his pets: he had seen the face of Christ in a man so trans- figured in prayer that the right order of creation was in him restored. For Bede St. Cuthbert . . . was the New Adam, once more at peace with all creation, naming the animals, who were the first servant and the first friend.[22]

As I read stories about these lives and see the place that the wild creatures play in them, I find myself thinking about the

mystery of coinherence, which I do not yet even begin to fully grasp or understand, by which the creator and the whole of the created universe, both human and nonhuman, are integrated into one whole living unity, part of common creation that links heaven and earth, humankind and all sentient beings.

But the hermit isolation was also broken in a much more thoroughly practical way. It was always clearly established that the hermit was connected to a community. This was a safeguard, and again if we are to appreciate what Merton's life can tell us, it is that he remained an essential part of the life of his brothers in the monastery of Gethsemani. In fact, many of these men were hermits either for a part of their lives, or were seasonal hermits, retiring to a cave or hut for a specific time, Advent or Lent, for example, so that the solitude became a means of empowering and refreshing their engagement with the world. We are told that St. Cuthbert left the demands of the monastery of Lindisfarne and set out "in deep delight toward that secret solitude for which he had so long desired and sought and striven. The coming and going of the active life had done its long work upon him, and he rejoiced that now he had earned his right to climb to the quiet of meditation upon God."[23] This, of course, makes the Celtic hermit life much more practical and relevant to my own. It reassures me that it is both right and possible to hold together the external demands and expectations of others and my own need to withdraw in order to find space and time in the cave of my heart to be alone with God. And then, in that time alone, the Celtic hermits show me much about mindfulness and awareness; about honesty toward the dark side of myself as well as the light; about the vital role that framework and structure must play; and above all about the role of praise, encouraging me to let the Psalms become as creative in my life as they were in theirs.

7

DARK FORCES

THE HERMIT IN his or her cell, intensely alive both to the beauty and the pain within and around, gives me a model that helps me to find in myself not only the joyous and affirmative but also the frightened, the sorrowful. I have little time for any sort of tradition that presents me with a "spirituality without tears," for I find that patronizing, demeaning. I resonated with what Dennis Potter, the playwright, said just a few months before his death from cancer: "Thank God religion to me has always been the wound, not the bandage."[1] My life has been rich but it has also had many times of desolation and depression when I have not been able to believe that there was any light at the end of the tunnel, when it was merely mockery to be told by well-intentioned friends that all would be well. I know that I have to face, and to live with, not only the dark forces in today's world, the suffering and injustice that is brought daily to me by the media, but also the dark forces that reign and have such power within my own self. None of us can evade the darkness.

Two contemporary Celtic writers, one from Scotland and one from Wales, have given me images in their writing that have helped me to appreciate the way in which one cannot hope to stay in the Garden of Eden, in a paradise where all seems well. George McLeod has written in one of his poems (which is surely really also a prayer) "In the garden always the thorn," for he knows the power of sin and how we are all caught up into that. He celebrates the creator and how gladly we live in the garden of his creation, "but creation is not enough."

> *In the garden also*
> *always the thorn.*
> *Creation is not enough.*
>
> *Almighty God Redeemer:*
> *The sap of life in our bones and being is Yours,*
> *lifting us to ecstasy.*
> *But always in the beauty the tang of sin . . .²*

The title in itself, *The Opened Door,* which Patrick Thomas uses for his small book on Celtic spirituality, presents me with another, equally meaningful picture. He tells the legend (which he has taken from the *Mabinogion)* of seven survivors of a Welsh expedition to Ireland who come to the island of Gwales, Grassholm, off the Pembrokeshire coast, to a great hall in a palace overlooking the sea. Two doors are open, and one is closed, the door that they must not open. There they live happily for eighty years, "and not withstanding that they themselves had suffered, there came to them no remembrance either of that or of any sorrow in the world," a joyous and delightful time, until one of them opens the forbidden door. "And when he looked, they were as conscious of every loss they had ever sustained, and of every kinsman and friend they had missed, and of every ill that had come upon them . . ." And then Patrick Thomas goes on to say that David Gwenallt Jones, one of the greatest modern Welsh poets, sees the opening of this door as a blessing rather than a betrayal. That open door ends any escapist hedonism, and instead forces the facing of the anguish of suffering humanity and the need to help it in its pain and misery, help that is to come from "the bread, the wine and the Cross."

Perhaps the Celtic tradition can help us all here particularly well because Celtic peoples themselves know suffering, personal and corporate suffering, better than most. A priest in the Church of Wales today asks what it is that the Irish, Scottish, and Welsh traditions have in common, and replies that they have all lived under the threat of extinction, yet they have survived. They have experienced virtually every form of suffering—social, economic, political, cultural—exile, insecurity, economic deprivation, political oppression. The countries of Ireland, Wales, and Scotland have seen moments of what must have seemed like total defeat: the death of Llewellyn in 1282 in Wales, for example. R. S. Thomas has summed up the Welsh experience: "We fought and were always in retreat." And yet the folk singer Dafydd Iwan, in a song commemorating sixteen hundred years of Welsh history, can say "In spite of everything, we are still here."[3]

A contemporary Welsh poet, Gillian Clarke, sits on the edge of the Llyn peninsula, in the far northwest of Wales, and she writes looking across the sea to Ireland:

Facing west, we've talked for hours
of our history,
thinking of Ireland and the hurt
cities,
gunshot on lonely farms . . .[4]

In 1848 the potato famine almost decimated Ireland, adding yet another dimension to the extreme sufferings of the Irish peoples. William Drennan crystalizes the anguish of the Irish people in these lines:

Hapless nation, rent and torn,
Thou were early taught to mourn;
Warfare of six hundred years!
Epochs marked with blood and tears!

Hapless nation! hapless land!
Heap of uncemented sand!
Crumbled by a foreign weight;
And by worse, domestic hate . . .

Here we watch our brother's sleep;
Watch with us, but no not weep;
Watch with us thro' dead of night—
But expect the morning light.[5]

When I was asked to go to South Africa, in the years when that country was still under apartheid, to talk to a gathering of Christian peoples of all denominations who were thinking about the future of the Church, I realized that it was to the Celtic tradition that I could point them. For while it brings no easy assurance, there is yet the promise of hope, hope against hope. Out of their long experience of living under threat, the Celtic nations remind us to "expect the morning light." Light in darkness, hope in despair, life in death, is their constant theme. These simple lines have been handed down from one generation to the next so that it is quite impossible to date them, and that in some strange way seems to make them more vividly the expression of a common shared heritage:

> *It is better to light a candle*
> *Than to curse the darkness.*[6]

The connection between suffering and creation is something that all early peoples knew as an essential part of their lives. In the seasonal cycle of the dying of the seed and the growth into new life, the farmer has to cut into the earth with his plow and he has to harrow the soil—even the words themselves for sowing carry the connotation of pain. In the human life cycle, pain is part of childbirth, as any mother can testify. Yet many people today, in trying to recover their Celtic roots, seem to be looking for some creation-centered spirituality that idealizes nature and presents some romantic idyll of the past. The reality would have been far different and it is vitally important to realize this. Nature can be cruel, uncertain, menacing. How often would the hermit, rising early to prayer on a beautiful summer's morning not find a cobweb at the entrance to the cell with a fly caught in it, victim of the spider's predatory instincts?

Surely St. Kevin cannot have failed to notice that his friend the otter apparently had no compunction in daily catching and bringing him a salmon from the lake? The great chain of being in the natural world is also a chain of creatures preying one on another, and while in one breath the monastic poet celebrates the elements as showing forth the harmony and the order of the creator God, he also has no illusions about its being a world that threatens and destroys.

This is a fallen world. Many of the Irish high crosses show Adam and Eve sharing the apple in the garden of Eden. If the same cross also shows St. Antony and St. Paul sharing the loaf in the Egyptian desert, two people sharing that round loaf together as once two people shared that round apple, that suggests, to my mind at least, a wonderfully vivid symbolic representation of redemption parallel to the fall. Indeed, the whole story depicted on the carved friezes of these crosses is the story of a God who rescues his people, who saves them and who feeds them. At the center of the cross is the figure of *Christus Victor,* Christ triumphant, having done battle with the forces of evil (which the ancient world often depicted as external forces). The Christ who takes on these forces and defeats them holds out those victorious, wounded hands (often disproportionately huge hands) to bless the world of which he is simultaneously both creator and redeemer. So the ultimate victory is won. Much of the early writing on the victory of the cross reflects a heroic age. The language is that of the heroic warrior who protects the community through his sword. A tenth-century poem that depicts Christ as a conquering hero uses words of the secular heroic tradition. "God who defended us . . .

Terrible grief, God defended us when he took on flesh . . .
Through the cross blood-stained, came salvation to the
world."[7]

These crosses, like the early texts of Celtic Christianity
speak not in optimism but in hope; not out of some bland
assurance that everything is all right, but out of confidence
in the grace of God and in his power to save a fallen world.

But the fallenness of that world cannot be denied.

By a woman and a tree
the world first perished.[8]

Time and again on the crosses we find Adam and Eve with a
great branching tree, sometimes so weighted down with apples that it seems almost to enclose them—has it, I wonder,
become a weeping tree, knowing that it too is part of the
fall? In this tenth-century poem Eve speaks on behalf of the
whole human race, lamenting what happened in the garden,
and how sin, brokenness, failure have come into the world:

I am Eve; great Adam's wife; it is I that outraged
Jesus of old; it is I that stole heaven from my
children; by rights it is I that should have gone upon
the Tree.

The poem ends: "There would be no hell; there would be
no sorrow; there would be no fear, were it not for me."[9] In
the *Saltair na Rann* Adam plays his part fully in the fall.
He tells Eve that if they have now lost their blessings and are
now without fire, house, drink, food, or clothing, it is his

fault. He proposes to Eve that they do penance together in silence, and suggests what surely must reflect a Celtic monastic practice, that they stand up to their necks in water—Eve in the Tigris for thirty-three days and Adam in the Jordan for forty-seven:

> *Lift thy two hands every canonical hour*
> *towards the heavenly Lord of the nine grades:*
> *pray for forgiveness.*
>
> *Let us beseech the whole of the creatures*
> *formed by God through His pure mysteries,*
> *that they implore with us the King of Justice*
> *that our transgression be forgiven.*[10]

The theme of human betrayal is put into the mouth of Judas in another early poem:

> *Woe is me that I forsook my King;*
> *Evil was the deed to which I put my hand;*
> *Therefore shall I be forever*
> *Without peace and without gentle affection.*[11]

The final line of the verse that follows says, "Woe twice over, and woe, O God." Here is a real cry from the heart, a cry of contrition wrung out from the depths, by a man who now realizes the cost of his sin: the failure to love the Lord, his betrayal of love and trust.

In the Celtic world there was a great sense of sin, a deep

feeling of sorrow, of contrition. But it is never the sense of guilt that so bedeviled my own childhood and brought a feeling of always being under judgment, of not being good enough, of failing time and again, however hard I might try. I even imposed upon myself all sorts of rituals and secret observances to try to placate this God, this all-seeing God, who was so strangely like my own patriarchal father. There is none of this here. I have found sorrow, deep sorrow, many tears, a real outpouring of grief, but it is never turned in on itself, never the kind of sorrow that becomes inward, self-destructive guilt, feeding on itself. Tears, as I learn them from the Celtic tradition, are never what so often my own tears become: tears of rage or of self-pity, tears of frustration, tears because I have put my own self at the center of the picture and feel that I have not received the treatment that I deserve—the tears of the child, in fact, for whom "life isn't fair"! There are tears of loss too, of bereavement, when I find myself caught into the past, clinging when I should learn to let go and to move on into the future. Here again there is the danger that what should be a purifying grief has become an inward-looking grieving whose concern is my own welfare and comfort. But true tears are those of real, deep personal sorrow, of repentance, that lead to the determination to change (which are, of course, what *metanoia* and "conversion" mean in the monastic tradition).

> *Grant me tears, O Lord, to blot out my sins; may I not cease from them, O God, until I have been purified.*

May my heart be burned by the fire of redemption;
  grant me tears with purity for Mary and Ite.

When I contemplate my sins, grant me tears always,
  for great are the claims of tears on cheeks.

Grant me tears when rising, grant me tears when
  resting, beyond your every gift altogether for love
  of you, Mary's Son.

Grant me tears in bed to moisten my pillow, so that
  his dear one may help to cure the soul.

Grant me contrition so that I may not be in disgrace;
  O Lord, protect me and grant me tears.

For the dalliance I had with women, who did not
  reject me, grant me tears, O Creator, flowing in
  streams from my eyes.

For my anger and my jealousy and my pride, a
  foolish deed, in pools from my inmost parts bring
  forth tears.

My falsehoods and my lying and my greed, grievous
  the three, to banish them all from me, O Mary
  grant me tears.[12]

A twelfth-century poem asks God for the gift of tears, for "a well of tears," for "fierce floods of tears."[13] These are tears that are freeing, cleansing. This is the sorrow that makes for healing, the sorrow that leads to joy. This is something that the monastic life understands well, and once again I find that I can fully appreciate Celtic spirituality only when I put it into its monastic context. The discovery of the wonderful concept of *compunction* has given me much strength and encouragement.[14] The word itself carries all sorts of resonances, for its root is *punctio*, which means literally to touch, pierce, prick. It carries a sensation of being pierced, stung, pricked, feeling a sharp stabbing pain. Compunction describes the experience of being touched or pierced by the awareness of my true state before God, and in the light of that awareness I am aroused from my drift, from lethargy, from complacency or denial. Now in the face of God's unconditional love and forgiveness I look with dismay on my own shortcomings, failings, above all my rejection of that love, yet never in a way that will trap me in yet more inward-looking self-analysis or introspection. Instead, I see that I have been false to my truest self, and that it is with my own self that the fault lies: I can blame no one else (point a finger at my parents, the environment, the institutional Church, contemporary society, which can be so tempting!). My feelings are stirred at my own compromising response to this outpouring of love and as a result I am roused up, spurred on, into taking action. It points me outward to trust in the mercy of God, reliance on his grace, and above all, response to his love. All the words that spring to mind are positive ones that suggest action. My heart has been pierced as if by a dart of love and I can hardly fail to respond.

Here is the sorrow that makes for joy. Here is the inner movement by which we turn from sin, from death within ourselves, liberating us from imprisonment within ourselves, a dying to self and an opening up into new life, new vision, more energy, renewed creativity. So the Celtic Church which is well known for its emphasis on penance, for its penitential literature, does not give us a gloomy Christianity. Here is the repentance that makes for joyous living. This is what true repentance brings: it sets me free to live fully, liberating me from the strangling cords of guilt. The intensity of the joyous sense of being alive is the other side of the ruthless acceptance of the recognition of sin. There is a most lovely thirteenth-century Welsh poem which is an expression of this. It has been called one of the greatest works of medieval Welsh literature. The heart of the poem is penance, and the desire for penance, but it is the penance that is the possibility of glory. This is the theme of the opening lines:

> *The beauty of virtue is doing penance for glory*
> *Beautiful too when God saves me.*

And the poem returns to this theme in its final lines:

> *Beautiful too doing penance for sin*
> *Most beautiful of all is honour and covenant*
> *With God on the Day of Judgment.*

In between comes a great outpouring, an exultant pleasure in the natural world, the sheer excitement of being alive in

God's world, and a sense of the goodness of that world. Here are some of the lines that most touched me:

> Summer and its days long and slow
> A herd of thick-maned horses
> The beauty of the word which the Trinity speaks
> Beautiful too when old age comes.[15]

I am grateful for the many litanylike prayers that express sorrow so magnificently and fully, repeating phrases and words time and time and time again, like the beating of the breast in sorrow. Many of these early Irish litanies are the products of private devotion. There is no hint that they were ever used, or intended to be used, in the public service of the church. They go on and on, petitioning again and again, heaping up verbs and epithets, abjuring and appealing to God:

> O Saviour of the human race;
> O true Physician of every disease, O heart-pitier and
>   assister of all misery;
> O fount of true purity and of true knowledge.[16]

The Godhead is addressed by every name and attribute:

> O true Priest, O true Physician, O true Prophet, O
>   true Friend,
>   Forgive.
> O only Sustainer of the Threefold mansion,
>   [i.e., heaven, earth, hell]

O only Life of all created things,
O only Light of the seven heavens,
   Forgive.
O Subject of the Scriptures meditation,
O Object of the chief prophets search,
O Marrow of true wisdom,
O Father of life,
O Voice of the people.
      Forgive.[17]

A litany of Jesus is wonderfully warm and vibrant, and I particularly enjoy the way in which the natural elements are used—heat, flame, sun, water—until at the end we come to human warmth and gentleness:

O holy Jesu:
O gentle friend;
O Morning Star;
O mid-day Sun adorned;
O brilliant flame of the righteous, and of
righteousness, and of everlasting life, and of eternity;
O Fountain ever-new, ever-living, ever-lasting; . . .
O true and loving brother;
O clement and friendly one.

This prayer for forgiveness, attributed to St. Ciaran, the sixth-century saint (though it is probably later), seems to be a personal devotional monastic prayer (using that word in its widest sense to include the laity as well) that may well have been prayed in the cross-vigil position, with arms stretched out horizontally.

"According to the multitude of your mercies, cleanse my iniquity."
> *O star-like sun,*
> *O guiding light,*
> *O home of the planets,*
> *O fiery-maned and marvellous One,*
> *O fertile, undulating, fiery sea,*
>> *Forgive.*

> *O fiery glow,*
> *O fiery flame of Judgment,*
>> *Forgive.*

> *O holy story-teller, holy scholar,*
> *O full of holy grace, of holy strength,*
> *O overflowing, loving, silent One,*
> *O generous and thunderous giver of gifts,*
>> *Forgive.*

> *O rock-like warrior of a hundred hosts,*
> *O fair crowned One, victorious, skilled in battle.*
>> *Forgive.*[18]

Here we can see the force of saying something again and again, how it unlocks something deep, how it is like the sea beating on us, wave after wave. It goes on and on. And what a canvas! It is a truly cosmic vision. All the elements of the whole created world are brought in, as though our own familiar world is not enough. There are so many images, such cascading words, such a cataract, as adjective succeeds adjective—and still we realize that God is beyond them all. Some of the images are quite startling in their originality. I love God being the "holy story-teller" or the "thunderous giver," and, of course, there is God the "warrior," the "victorious" one in that final verse. And yet all the time the prayer remains deeply personal and interior, and we should not miss the significance of the fact that it opens with a line from the Psalms. This is *lectio*, the monastic way of praying with a phrase from Scripture, repeating it, rocking it back and forward, letting it move into the depths of one's own self until it goes beyond words into silence, into contemplation.

Probably the most splendid of all the Irish litanies that I have found is that attributed to Mugron Abbot of the federated monastery of Iona and Durrow from 964–80. It is a litany of the Trinity, and brings me back once again to the Trinitarian understanding which is always so strong:

> *Have mercy upon us, O God the Father Almighty*
> *God of hosts*
> *O High God,*
> *O Lord of the world,*
> *O ineffable God,*
> *O Creator of the Elements,*
> *O invisible God,*

O incorporeal God,
O God beyond all judgement,
O impassible God,
O incorruptible God,
O immortal God,
O immoveable God,
O eternal God,
O perfect God,
O merciful God,
O wondrous God,
O dreadful God,
O God of the earth,
O God of fire,
O God of the excellent waters,
O God of the tempestuous and rushing air,
O God of the many languages round the circuit of
   the earth,
O God of the waves from the bottomless house of the
   ocean,
O God of the constellations, and all the bright stars,
O God who didst fashion the mass, and didst
   inaugurate day and night,
O God who didst rule over hell, and its rabble host,
O God who dost govern with archangels,
O golden good,
O heavenly Father who are in heaven,
     Have mercy upon us.[19]

When I say this litany or sing it or pray it, its great scope embracing the whole universe seems to bring a vast and wide span into my own inner landscape, and take me away from any danger of narrow or petty gazing at my own sins and weakness. In this amazing cosmic context, I am both uplifted and humbled before the majestic presence of the Godhead.

Unless we appreciate the deeply ascetic strand that runs throughout Celtic Christianity we cannot do justice to the fullness of the Celtic tradition. Much is said of martyrdom, in three kinds, the red, the white, and the blue or green. The first is the generally accepted martyrdom of being killed for the faith. The second is renunciation of the world, the way of exile, or *peregrinatio*, which can by definition be the vocation of only a chosen few. But the third, the blue or the green, devotion to austerities, can be pursued by anyone; it is the life of denial, of daily repentance, hidden, secret, which can be experienced without leaving home, and which is essentially about the disposition of the heart, bringing body and mind under control so that men and women can serve God more fully and freely.

There were three Lents in the Celtic Church, not only the Lent that we know, but one before Christmas and another after Pentecost. It was the Lent of Elijah in winter, of Jesus in the spring, and of Moses in the summer. In addition, penitential fasting was practiced not only on Fridays but also on Wednesdays. The way in which private confession and penance developed in the Celtic Church made a very particular and peculiar contribution to the understanding of the wider Church. Penance had, of course, been practiced in the Church in Europe, but it was public penance, something that tended to isolate and humiliate and demean. Penitents became the lowest of the low, excluded from the main body of the Church, and charged with such unpleasant duties as the carrying of corpses. Private penance, however, made much more obvious the aim and purpose of penance, not punitive or vindictive but remedial. Confession and penance were "medicine for souls," intended to heal the hurt men and women did by sin, primarily the hurt to themselves but also the hurt to society.

The confessor was a "soul-friend," *anamchara* in Irish, *periglour* in Welsh, whose work was to apply the appropriate cure to the soul's disease. "Diversity of offenses causes diversity of penance." Here is the work of the spiritual doctor curing the wounds of the soul, restoring what is weak to a complete state of health. Christ himself is, of course, the physician, but it is the soul-friend who has to impose an appropriate penance after the confession of sins. The books called penitentials are tariffs setting out how for each sin there is a corresponding penance, consisting of the recitation of Psalms, corporal punishment, fasting on bread and water. Four Welsh texts of the early sixth century are the earliest documents that we have, the Irish follow. One of the Welsh texts was taken to Brittany and by the eighth century all the texts were circulating in Europe.[20]

It might be tempting to pick out at random some of the more extraordinary examples and hold them up to ridicule. "If someone argues with a cleric or minister of God, he will fast for a week on bread and water." "If a cleric has once or twice committed a theft by stealing a sheep, a pig, or another animal, he will fast for one year on bread and water and will pay back what he has stolen fourfold." But this is to miss their underlying purpose. Their grasp of the workings of the human psyche is well shown in the way in which the eight chief virtues are opposed to the eight chief vices in order to cure and heal them: moderation versus gluttony and drunkenness; generosity versus avarice; benevolence of heart versus envy and hatred; humility versus pride. There is always a sense of growth and movement, very much in line with what we know today as necessary for the health of mind, body, and soul.

As I read what was written in these penitentials, I find much that is vivid and honest, and which strikes a chord. On anger: "as the edge of a weapon pierces a man's body so the sharp point of anger pierces the soul and causes its death." On avarice: "it may be compared to Hell as to its extent and capacity, and because it gives up nothing that is cast into it, so likewise the maw of avarice, though the whole world's wealth were poured into it, could not be filled, and would give nothing back again." Or envy: "the nature of envy, with malice, is likened to the nature of fire. For it is the way of fire that it burns indifferently what is below and above and about it . . . So also envy assails."

It is the soul-friend who helps above all, who brings medicine for the soul, who supports and who challenges throughout one's life. The soul-friend is unique to the Celtic Church though clearly it owes much to both the desert tradition and Druidic practices. According to Nora Chadwick, the rise of the *anamchara* in the Celtic Churches was a natural development from the *syncellus,* the "one who shares a cell" in the desert tradition, and to whom one confessed, revealing confidential aspects of one's life. The cell, wherever it may be found in the early years of the Church, whether in the Egyptian desert or in remoter areas of any of the Celtic countries, is the place of encounter with God and one's true self and the world, and thus the sharing of the cell is the sharing of one's inmost self, heart, and mind.[21] Here is the truest and deepest form of friendship, what the desert guides called *exagoreusis,* that opening of one's heart to another which leads to *hesychia,* serenity and peace of heart.

The importance of everyone, cleric and lay, male and female, having a soul-friend, is a tacit acknowledgment of the role of a spiritual mentor and of the deep human need for the experience of reconciliation and healing. The point is made apparent in the often-quoted story of St. Brigit found in the early ninth-century *Martyrology of Oengus the Culdee,* which tells of a young foster son of hers eating with her in the refectory. When she asks him whether he has a soul-friend he immediately says that of course he has, but St. Brigit replies:

"let us sing his requiem": for she saw, while the young man was still eating, that he had died, and from that moment she watched the young man's food being put directly into the trunk of his body since he was now without a head. "Go forth and eat nothing until you get a soul-friend, for anyone without a soul-friend is like a body without a head; is like the water of a polluted lake, neither good for drinking nor for washing. That is the person without a soul-friend."[22]

The setting is dramatic enough, the sacramental allusions, the image of water, all speak for themselves. This role of the soul-friend is of the utmost importance.

How seriously this is taken is apparent in a saying attributed to Maelruain, the *Rule of the Céile Dé*, which warns: "Any person who does not reverence the rule of the soul-friend is not in harmony with God or man . . ." Maelruain, the founder and abbot of the monastery of Tallaght, was a leading figure in the eighth-century reform movement the Céile Dé which encouraged the eremitical life and sought to bring monasticism back to a greater austerity and asceticism. He died in 792 and was himself very important as soul-friend to many influential men of the following generation, not least Oengus the Culdee (died 824). *The Martyrology,* which Oengus composed at Tallaght, calls Maelruain "the splendid sun of the Gaels' island." This soul-friendship with him clearly lasted not only throughout his lifetime but beyond it, for he tells us that a visit to his grave "heals the sighs of my heart" and that he still continued to pray to him for guidance:

May my tutor bring me unto Christ
Dear beyond affection
By his pure blessing
with his heart's desire.[23]

The relationship of soul-friendship existed between men and women, women and women, men and men, cleric and lay. The soul-friend was the spiritual guide who helped everyone to find his or her own path. The practice of seeing one's soul-friend on a regular basis seems to have been expected by all who committed themselves to the relationship. Maelruain was very clear about this. Consultation should occur at least once a year but "if he be nearer consult him oftener." It was true friendship, with warmth and intimacy and honesty, and there is a profound respect for the other's wisdom, despite age or gender differences, as the source of blessing. But it was not merely affirmative. This is, much more than what so often the modern reduction has made of it, finding someone to "share the journey—walk the path." There is challenge as well, confrontation, not collusion. Again Maelruain is quite clear: "When you put yourself under the judgment or control of another, seek out the fire that you think will burn you most keenly, that is, him or her who will least spare you." Nor is there to be any wandering around from one soul-friend to another since this can so easily lead to superficial relationships and the likelihood of contradictory advice. Any previous relationship has to be terminated when the new one starts, as with an apprentice, since the artisan or craftsman "does not like a man of his household to go to anyone else"—in the words of a conversation in which the soul-friend checks on whether permission has been sought for this new relationship. For it is the fullness and the honesty of the confession that makes the system work. The principle is enunciated in a story about a soul-friend named Helair. "This is what Helair did in the matter; at first he had received many penitents but he ended by sending them all away because he saw that their penance was not zealously performed, and also that they concealed their sins when making confession."[24]

The Celtic approach to penance has been called a landmark in the development of a compassionate pastoral approach toward personal sin in the Latin West. It recognizes sin and refuses to deny the dark, but only in order that the sinner may be helped to move forward in real acceptance and honesty. Once again it reminds us of the corporate nature of Celtic spirituality, the recognition of our need for and dependence on one another. God is, of course, the ultimate soul-friend, but it is as though he had his lieutenants or helpers along the way. So once again we are taken into the mystery of interconnectedness, or interrelatedness, which the Celtic peoples knew so well and which they tell us that we also need.

8

THE CROSS

TIME AND AGAIN the modern Welsh poet David Gwenallt Jones makes reference to the cross in his poems, for it is part of the world that he knows. He talks of St. David walking among us today, coming into the schools and mines and factories, and finally into our own homes, putting the holy vessels on the kitchen table, with bread from the pantry and wine from the cellar, and after communion talking around the fire:

> And he spoke to us of God's natural order.
> The person, the family, the nation, and the society of
>   nations
> And the cross which prevents us from making any of
>   them into a god.[1]

When he writes of the way in which the old hymns shaped his spiritual life, he tells us that they brought "the crib, the Cross, the empty grave and Pentecost back again, firely new." His poem "The Door" has the phrase "and we saw the bread, the wine and Cross" and he makes the context clear: "the cry of the country in its pain, the red barking of the industrial dust, and saw the bread, the wine and the Cross."[2] He puts the Eucharist and the cross brutally into the suffering of his own times, into the social and economic dislocation of the valleys of South Wales that he knew well, so that what might otherwise be helplessness and despair is transformed into hope.

Here we see the role of the cross in contemporary Welsh spirituality. But the cross has always been at the heart of the religious understanding of Celtic peoples. The power of the cross in the Celtic tradition is immediately apparent to anyone exploring Celtic countries, for we find that each has its own peculiar form. Wales had many magnificent decorated and sculpted crosses, the Isle of Man crosses with extraordinary and unique carving, often showing pagan Viking influence, the smaller crosses of Cornwall proliferate, scattered, often almost hidden. In Ireland the high crosses first appear in the eighth century with nonrepresentational interlacing geometric designs, and from this develops the Scriptural crosses, amazing masterpieces of skill and imagination that we can still see in Clonmacnois, Moone, or Monasterboice. Throughout history stone has always carried a religious significance and the Celtic peoples recognized this as they took something vitally important in the pre-Christian world and brought it into the new world of Christianity. When they placed these standing stone crosses so prominently in the landscape, they were saying something about the place of the cross in their lives. Here, in the words of Patrick Thomas, is "Celtic Christian stonework with the message of creation restored and made whole by the cross of Christ."[3]

The first time that I stood in front of an Irish high cross was a moment of conversion, for I then saw just how far the Celtic tradition carried a power that went far beyond words.

The high cross at Monasterboice (the cross of Muiredach, an abbot who died in 923) has a succession of panels, intricately carved, infused with vigor and vibrant energy. They show scenes from the Old and New Testaments as well as St. Antony and St. Paul sharing bread in the wilderness, with interlacing spirals and vine scrolls. The figure of Christ on the cross is the center on which everything converges. Christ reigns from the cross, triumphant over the powers and evil which he has defeated. "By death he has trampled down death," in the wonderful words of the proclamation in the Orthodox Easter night service.

Here it becomes impossible to deny the centrality of the cross. I am unhappy with the use of the phrase "creation-centered spirituality" and would rather speak of "creation-filled spirituality." The Celtic celebration of creation is unparalleled in its glorious enjoyment of the whole created universe and this is without doubt one of their greatest gifts to us. But in a Celtic cross we see that great round O, the circle of the globe itself, held in tension by the two arms of the cross—creation and redemption together. There is much scholarly discussion about the origins of this unique shape, found only in Celtic countries. Does it derive from the victor's laurel wreath hung on the Roman standard? Does it come from a wooden prototype in which the arcs joining the arms would strengthen it as it was carried in procession? Is there any connection between the circle and Druidic worship? Is the circle the sun of Easter shining through the dark icon of the crucifixion, as Noel Dermott O'Donoghue suggests?[4] If the crosses were painted, which almost certainly they were, might not the ring-arcs have been the colors of the rainbow, a reminder of the rainbow of the covenant? Perhaps the circle is itself the halo of the glory of Christ, in which case to stand before a cross is to stand in the very presence of Christ himself. In this case the cross does not merely speak of Christ, it *is* Christ himself, risen and glorified. I draw back at this point, unwilling to analyze or interpret too much. In the end I am quite happy not to know.

But then, what about those beautiful decorative patterns, those intricate designs of spirals and interlacings that are so much a part of these crosses? They are a fascinating play with nonrepresentational forms that do not "depict" anything. Might these patterns have been of meditative import? Was this perhaps the intention? Is it possible that like mandalas, they bring us abstract forms to encourage meditation? The circle and the unending interlace seem to speak of God's unity and eternity, the interlocking forms suggest the order underlying the complexity of creation. If there is a lozenge, may it not stand for Christ, the second person of the Trinity, the *logos*? The daily monastic practice of *lectio divina*, taking a phrase from Scripture, staying with it, praying with it, turning it over and over again in the mind and heart until it takes one beyond words—might the crosses have played their part in this? Like the Psalms, they speak of continuity, eternity, order, and growth, unity within complexity.[5]

Raised bosses, or knobs in high relief, appear widely, for example on the south cross at Clonmacnois, where a magnificent panel of eight bosses on the east side of the main shaft balances a crucifixion scene on the west face.

Sometimes the circle surrounding the crucifixion or the Last Judgment will contain four studs, like the four points of the compass pointing in four directions. Here we enter the world of number symbolism, the language of numbers, without which we cannot fully appreciate the power and presence of these crosses and the wealth of mystical thinking and theology that they hold. The symbolic association of numbers and measurement would have been particularly congenial to a people who delighted in numbers and derivations and who enjoyed multiple interpretations and layers of meaning.[6] The treatise on the Mass at the end of the Stowe Missal, dated around the year 800, has much to say on the meaning of numbers, and the ninth-century Irish philosopher, John Scotus Erigena, in his *On the Division of Nature,* made the works of the Neoplatonists available to the West, which established a system of celestial arithmetic allied to scriptural exegesis by which a divine plan for the universe was expressed in numbers, geometry, and measurement. The number five symbolizing the wounds of Christ is, of course, generally familiar because of the five consecration crosses on an altar. Five is not only a reminder of the loaves in the feeding of the five thousand but also the five books of the Mosaic law which nourish men and women. Twelve has its obvious association with the apostles, while four is the number of the evangelists. There were two fishes as well as five barley loaves, as there are both prophets and psalmists, Old and New Testaments. The number eight is the number of perfect harmony bringing together the five human senses with the three members of the Godhead. How many meanings would the eye of the heart, not merely the physical eye, see? We cannot tell. But as Hilary Richardson, who has made this a particular study, has said, "multiple interpretations, ambiguities and half-glimpsed perceptions continued their centuries-old native tradition."[7]

We know that it was common in early Christian Ireland for almost every church to have a cross near it and we know from references in monastic rules that it had a liturgical use with daily prayer being performed at the cross. The eighth-century rule of Ailbe says, "After the head-monk [the abbot] to the cross with gentle choir-singing, with strong streams of tears from righteous cheeks." Br. Eoin de Bhaldraithe tells us that this was in imitation of the daily office sung in Jerusalem at the Church of the Resurrection, when people gathered for what they called a celebration of light which we today call vespers. Psalms were sung at the church itself and with the singing of further hymns they would process to the place of Golgotha, an ornamental metal cross set on a rock outside the door. (The earliest Irish crosses placed on a heap of stones, or those with a huge single rock forming the base, recalled Golgotha.) Here more hymns would be sung, and prayers said in front and behind the cross, as people moved all around it, praying and singing. It seems that the cross was itself an object of devotion, but beyond that we must remain open, as Eamonn O'Corrigan reminds us, to the possibility "that patrons or sculptors, trained in liturgical action and *lectio divina* may have designed their crosses to embody the multiple levels of meaning which onlookers with different levels of education and different interests would seek."[8]

One thing is clear, however, and that is that these crosses must have stood as a focal point in the countryside, claiming the land for Christ, making a statement of belief in the possibility of a transfigured universe. Everything centers on the crucified Christ at the center of the cross, which is always stark. We see a suffering Christ, and the two figures standing on either side are a part of the humanity implicated in that suffering. On the right hand there is always Longinus, plunging his sword into Christ's side, and on the right Stephaton, holding a long pole at the end of which there is the bitter drink, gall or vinegar, two events which did not, of course, happen at the same time. But that is not the point. They are chosen partly for their symmetrical composition but more important for their symbolic meaning. The lance bearer is seen to represent the church and the sponge bearer the synagogue, since according to legend, from Christ's side poured out blood and water which healed the blindness of Longinus—and makes the contrast between the sacraments of the church and the bitter gall of the Jewish faith. The persons of Mary or St. John are never present, no mother or close friend. There is nothing here approaching the softness, sometimes close to sentimentality, found in the Middle Ages, though sometimes there are angels close to Christ's head. This is heroic suffering. This is Christ as hero, in the old tradition of the heroic as it is found in Celtic myth and legend, the hero who does not flinch from the ordeal of personal destruction in order to save his people.

Sometimes, however, the figure of the crucified Christ is simultaneously that of the risen Lord, shown in the long white robe of Easter. Here death and resurrection, Good

Friday and Easter, become one. Much in these carvings speak in images which, as Tillich says, give "no objective knowledge but a true insight." The symbolism of these crosses allows each of us to go as far as we want, or as far as we are able. I believe that the longer we stay with these images, the more profound will their resonance become, and I am myself deeply grateful for the way in which these crosses have over time become a kind of visual *lectio divina*, their meaning yielded up only with attention and with prayer.

On the opposite side of the cross we are shown Christ as the Lord of Hosts, at the Second Coming, on the Day of Judgment. It is a vigorous portrayal with the blessed, the saved, in a dense crowd on Christ's right hand, and on his left the damned being dispatched by two devils, one wielding a fork and the other holding a book and frequently giving a mighty kick to those nearest him. In a small panel below, St. Michael is holding the scales with which he weighs a small human figure. Christ himself is striking, for he is standing erect, holding a cross in his left hand and in his right a flowering rod or bough, the two stems crossed in front of him. This motif is clearly that of Osiris-judge, and so another reminder of the Celtic link with Egypt and the East, for this is found in the *Books of the Dead* of pre-Christian Egypt. Here again is a vivid image: the flowering bough which speaks of the resurrection, and of new life in Christ.

"O Tree whose blossoms never fail." The visual representation in the crosses finds verbal expression in Celtic poetry, hymns, and blessings. This phrase comes from what

Douglas Hyde describes as the verse-prayers men and women would recite each night three times before going to sleep.[9] As he traveled through Ireland at the end of the last century, he found that the passion of Christ was the cornerstone of the people's faith. He collected numbers of such prayers, "simple, humble hopeful cries," he called them, one of which was given to him by a schoolmaster in County Cork, and opens:

> *In the name of the Father it is I come to rest,*
> *lying on my bed in Thy name,*
> *O noble King.*

And it ends:

> *I place the tree upon which Christ was crucified*
> *Between me and the heavy-lying night-mare*
> *Between me and each evil-thing.*

In Scotland at the same time Alexander Carmichael found many similar prayers with lines such as these:

> *Thou Christ of the tree,*
>   *Thou Christ of the cross.*[10]

Another Irish night-prayer addresses God:

> *O King of the wounds*
> *Who wast crucified on the tree.*[11]

For of course the historical cross standing on the hill out-side Jerusalem would have been of wood, a wooden cross cut from a living tree. As the human race fell by a tree, so also was mankind redeemed by a tree. There was much play with the idea that men and women having fallen through the fruits of a tree were also redeemed by a tree. In the words of one medieval theologian, Fulbert of Chartres: "By hanging from a cross with a tree's help he took away the poison that came from a tree. And opened again the closed doors to life." So the tree plays an important part in the living tradition of the cross, and in this, once again, Christianity is found taking up into itself something that was very important in pre-Christian religion, something deep and universal, and again probably something that retains great significance for numbers of people today even if they hardly acknowledge it consciously. For our ancestors, trees were not merely natural objects, they were majestic signs of the connectedness of the heaven and the earth. They saw the pattern of the immense root system that bound the tree to the earth, and then above it that immense system of arms and handlike leaves stretching out into the sky above, and the trunk itself standing there so strongly, the axis that bound the underworld with the upperworld, the human with the divine, the earthly with the spiritual, the world itself with God. So when Christ was lifted up from the earth and displayed spreadeagled on a dead tree set up on a hill, the ancient archetype of the tree of life suddenly blazed out in living historical actuality, fulfilled once and for all, and the primeval myth of the sacred tree-ladder connecting God with the world, the divine with the earthly, suddenly found real and historical expression—for there is an actual tree, the cross of the crucifixion, connecting us with God and God with us, once and for all, in the figure of Christ—Christ the axis of history.

According to Welsh tradition, the tree of the crucifixion was a rowan, which is why the berries of the rowan look like drops of blood.[12] But in Scotland Carmichael was told that it was the aspen that "was chosen by the enemies of Christ for the cross upon which to crucify the Saviour of mankind." That is why it was hated so much and why no crofter in Uist would use its wood for his plow or harrow or any of his farm implements, and no fisherman would use it in his boat or for any of his fishing gear. Still to this day its leaves hang their heads and shake for shame. "Hence the ever-tremulous, ever-quivering, ever-quaking motion of the guilty hateful aspen even in the stillest air" and why people continue to hurl at it clods and stones and other missiles as well as curses.[13]

Much Celtic poetic writing about the cross is extraordinarily vivid, original, and, I feel, unparalleled elsewhere. What I have found totally unique is the prayer-poem known as the "Virgin's Dream," or the "Dream of Mary," used as a daily personal devotion among the Welsh, the Irish, and the Breton of the last century, but again undoubtedly handed down in oral tradition from a distant past. It takes the form of a conversation between Mary and either the apostles or Jesus himself. In *Poem-Book of the Gael* it is called "The keening of Mary." It is Mary who speaks first:

O Peter, O Apostle, has thou seen my bright love?

I saw Him even now in the midst of His foemen

Who is that stately man on the tree of the Passion?

Dost thou not know thy son, O Mother?

And is that the little son I carried nine months?
And is that the little son that was born in the stable?
And is that the little son that was nursed at Mary's
  breast?

Hush O Mother and be not sorrowful.

And then Mary addresses Christ on the cross:

And is that the hammer that struck home nails
  through thee?
And is that the spear that went through thy white
  side?
And is that the crown of thorns that crowned thy
  beauteous head?

Hush O Mother and be not sorrowful.

According to Eleanor Hull this was taken down from Mary Clancy of Moycullen, who keened it with great sobbing in her voice, in a low recitative.[14]

In the last century, James Fisher, who translated

Breuddwyd Mair, the "Virgin's Dream," from many parts of Wales, said that it was widely known and repeated kneeling, and felt to be more important to the people than either the Lord's Prayer or the Creed. He collected ten versions and commented that it was hardly surprising that there should be such variations since it represented a devotion dating from pre-Reformation times passed down in oral transmission. He said that if the schoolchildren in the neighborhood of Tywyn in Merionethshire, about 1850–60, were asked if they knew the *Gweddi'r Forwyn*, as it was known there, "something like half their number in the upper classes would probably have held up their hands."[15] Here the dialogue is between Mary and Christ, and he speaks first:

> *Blessed Mother Mary, art Thou sleeping?*
>
> *Yes, my dear Son, I am dreaming.*
>
> *Blessed Mother, what dost thou see in thy dream?*
>
> *I see thee pursued, and followed, and taken,*
> *And placed up the Cross,*
> *And Thy hands and Thy feet nailed;*
> *A blind, dark man, deceived of the Evil One,*
> *With the point of his spear is piercing Thee*
> *Under thy right breast,*
> *And all Thy blessed blood is being shed . . .*

Similar poems were also current among the Breton-speaking peoples of lower Brittany, with interesting variants:

My dear son, I see
That you will be arrested to-night
By men carrying a bright closed lantern;
You will be nailed upon a cross,
And scourged with whips;
They will spit upon your sacred face;
You will be trodden down and spurned by the foot.[16]

I find here the same tenderness of feeling and immediacy of detail as with Blathmac, the monastic poet, writing in Ireland in the eighth century. When he retells the biblical story as a long narrative poem, at one point he is speaking to Mary and sharing her grief:

Come to me, loving Mary,
That I may keen with you your very dear one.
Alas! the going to the cross of your son,
That great jewel, that beautiful champion.

Then, as he goes on to describe the scene of the crucifixion, it is as though he, and we too, are seeing it for the first time. And it is made the more poignant since he having spoken of Christ as a jewel, a champion, now addresses him as King, the King of the seven holy heavens, so that to watch Christ as King undergoing all these indignities is particularly pitiful:

A purple cloak was put upon the King by the ignoble
assembly; in mockery that was put about him, not
from a desire to cover him.

Hands were laid upon the face of the King who was severely chastised. Hideous deed—the face of the Creator was spat upon.

They offered him a parting drink, desiring that he should die soon; an unlawful deed, the mixed gall with vinegar for him.

He raised a soft reproachful voice, beseeching his holy father: "Why, O living God, hast Thou left me to my servitude and my suffering?"

But while this is deeply personal, "It is to save each person that my famous King has come," it is also cosmic. Blathmac speaks of the whole universe caught up into the suffering— an idea more common in the East, so that once again we are reminded of the very strong Eastern influence in the Celtic tradition:

The sun concealed its proper light; it lamented its lord. A swift cloud went across the blue sky, the great stormy sea roared.

The whole world became dark, great trembling came on the earth; at the death of noble Jesus great rocks burst open.

Jerusalem suddenly cast up the dead from ancient burial; in the hour in which Jesus suffered death the veil of the temple was rent.

A fierce stream of blood boiled until the bark of
every tree was red; there was blood throughout the
world in the tops of every great wood.

It would have been fitting for God's elements—the
fair sea, the blue sky, the earth—to have changed
their appearance, lamenting their calamity.

The body of Christ exposed to the spear-thrust
demanded harsh lamentation—that they should have
mourned more grievously the Man by whom they
were created.[17]

There is something comparable in the *Saltair na Ramm*:

Dear God's elements were afraid when the veil of the
    temple was rent. Every creature wailed—
Heaven and earth trembled:
The sea proceeded to go over its bounds:
Hearts of black rocks split.[18]

"The Cross of Christ about us" is a traditional Irish saying
that is still common today just as it was a hundred years ago
when Douglas Hyde was making his collection of the religious songs of Connacht and found that for these people
God was in their mouths and before their eyes, day and
night. When any sudden trouble came upon them, they
would say, "The Cross of Christ upon us." This poem was
probably originally medieval, though as with so much of

this material handed down in oral tradition it is quite impossible to date:

> Remember [or think of] the Cross each day,
>> And the King of the Graces who was raised
>> upon it.
> Think upon that and on His passion,
> Think forever of thy going into the tomb.

If the cross was central to life and belief, it was because of its immediate presence, a force that anyone can call upon in need. And so we find the continuation of the lorica, the breastplate or protection prayer that goes back in time to the Druids and, according to tradition, to its use by St. Patrick on Easter Eve in the year 433. What I like about it is that so often it has the quality of being totally specific, physical in the way in which it points to prayer for times of danger and uncertainty. Here is a tenth-century poem:

> Christ's Cross over this face, and thus over my ear.
> Christ's Cross over these eyes . . . this mouth . . .
> this throat . . . the back of this head . . . this side
> . . . to accompany before me . . . to accompany
> behind me . . . Christ's Cross to meet every
> difficulty both on hollow and on hill . . . Christ's
> Cross over my community. Christ's Cross over my
> church. Christ's Cross in the next world. Christ's
> Cross in this world.[19]

In this prayer, which is attributed to St. Fursa, one of the wandering saints of the eighth century, I watch him putting the whole of himself under God's protection in a way that encourages me to feel that I, as I use it, can ask for the strengthening of each part of my own body, commending each element in turn:

May the yoke of the Law of God be on this shoulder
May the coming of the Holy Spirit be on this head
May the sign of Christ be on this forehead
May the hearing of the Holy Spirit be in these ears
May the smelling of the Holy Spirit be in this nose
May the vision that the People of Heaven have be in these eyes
May the speech of the People of Heaven be in this mouth
May the work of the Church of God be in these hands
May the good of God and of the neighbour be in these feet
May God be dwelling in this heart
May this man belong entirely to God the Father.[20]

With these Celtic prayers I learn both to pray with the body and for the body, and I am grateful to be allowed to be so totally physical and not to feel that being holy or being spiritual involves denial of the body. It was common practice in the monasteries for praying to be accompanied by gestures of the body. In the Rule attributed to St. Comghall we read: "A hundred prostrations to Him at the *Biait* [i.e.,

Psalms 118–119, so called from the opening word *beati*] morning and evening." The *Rule of Ailbe* asks for one hundred genuflections at the *beati* at the beginning of the day and one hundred at vespers, at the end. Often genuflection was usual at the end of every Psalm. Sometimes praying took the form of the cross-vigil, praying with the arms fully extended—often for exceedingly long stretches at a time. The story of St. Kevin, praying with hands held out open and the blackbird coming and laying an egg on his open palm, must refer to this—and the fact that the legend tells that he went on praying, neither opening nor closing his hand until the eggs were hatched, only further enhances the point.[21] A gloss on Psalm 133 in a ninth-century collection tells how prayer involved the whole of the person. "The raising of the hands in cross-vigil, that is the word of the hands, and the word of the eyes, moreover, it is the raisings of them up to God, and the word of the knees and of the legs is the sending of them in prostration, and the word of the body, moreover, is when it is extended to God in prostration and cross-vigil."[22]

But then if I learn to pray with the body I also learn to pray for the body! These are prayers that ask God in quite clear and definite terms not to let into the body or into the being anything that can be harmful. They ask for God's protection for the whole human body, from the top of the head to the soles of the feet, both externally and internally; one prayer speaks of the five senses and the ten openings of the body. It was strongly felt that evil came into the body through the ten orifices, the tenth being entry through the head. The power of God was sought to protect all the points

of access into the body. Here is a prayer that speaks with a
tremendous assurance of God's presence and protecting
powers:

O God, hearken to my prayer
Let my earnest petition come to Thee,
For I know that Thou are hearing me
As surely as though I saw Thee with mine eyes . . .

Let no thought come to my heart,
Let no sound come to mine ear,
Let no temptation come to mine eye,
Let no fragrance come to my nose . . .

Let no fancy come to my mind
Let no ruffle come to my spirit,
That is hurtful to my body this night,
Nor ill for my soul at the hour of my death.[23]

It is the sense of touch which I so much appreciate in this
prayer addressed to Christ as the bringer of healing:

Put Thy salve to my sight,
Put Thy balm to my wounds,
Put Thy linen robe to my skin,
O Healing Hand, O Son of the God of salvation.[24]

Therefore, it is not surprising to find how many prayers
have this strong sense of physical presence, above all of a
loving arm or hand around one, particularly in going to

sleep at night. "Be Thy right hand, O God, under my head" is a very typical opening.[25] Here is the first verse of a bed-blessing at the end of the day which I love for its tender assurance:

> *I lie in my bed*
> *As I would lie in the grave,*
> *Thine arm beneath my neck,*
> *Thou Son of Mary victorious.*[26]

Encompassing prayers belong to another slightly different genre of praying, and were to be found both in Ireland and in Scotland. They often open by speaking of the arm or the hand of God: "The compassing of God and His right hand," for the idea of encircling or encompassing was very popular. The *"caim"* was a common form of safeguarding in which the persons of the Trinity or any of the saints, or Mary, would be invoked for protection of the person in need. It was done by stretching out the right hand with the forefinger extended and turning sunwise, as if on a pivot, describing a circle with the tip of the forefinger and as they did so, invoking "the sanctuary of God," "the encompassing of Christ," "the encircling of Mary," and so on. Then the circle encloses that person and accompanies them as they walk onward, safeguarding them from all evil without or within.[27]

> *The compassing of God and His right hand*
> *Be upon my form and upon my frame*

The compassing of the High King and the grace of
  the Trinity
Be upon me abiding ever eternally,
  Be upon me abiding ever eternally.[28]

In some places in Ireland Pochin Mould found the custom of making a protective lorica, or breastplate, by turning to the four points of the compass and making the sign of the cross at each. "First say the Lord's Prayer. Then face east, hands raised in the ancient position of prayer, say 'God come to my help, Lord make haste to help me.' Then make the sign of the cross and repeat the formula to four quarters, first with the eyes cast down, then looking up to heaven."[29]

All the time it is through the victory of the cross that protection is sought from the forces of fear, evil, distress:

May the cross of the crucifixion tree
  Upon the wounded back of Christ
Deliver me from distress,
  From death and from spells.

The cross of Christ without fault,
  All outstretched towards me;
O God, bless to me my lot
  Before my going out.

What harm soever may be therein
  May I not take thence,

For the sake of Christ the guileless,
  For the sake of the King of power.

In name of the King of life,
In name of the Christ of love,
In name of the Holy Spirit,
  The Triune of my strength.[30]

In this sleep prayer the suffering and sacrifice of the crucifixion are spoken of with complete assurance and a sort of sentimentality:

O Jesu without sin,
King of the poor,
Who were sorely subdued
Under the ban of the wicked,
Shield Thou me this night
  From Judas.

My soul on Thine own arm, O Christ,
Thou the King of the City of Heaven,
Thou it was who bought'st my soul O Jesu,
  Thou it was who didst sacrifice Thy life for me.

Protect Thou me because of my sorrow,
For the sake of Thy passion, Thy wounds, and Thy
  blood,
And take me in safety to-night
  Near to the City of God.[31]

9

THE SAINTS

CELTIC SAINTS ARE approachable, close at hand, woven quite naturally into life just as would be any other member of an extended family. It is this that sets them apart from the great saints of the Western Church, who were made saints by formal canonization through the process of a centralized ecclesiastical machinery. The saints of Europe will so often be known because of their relics, their corporal remains, their shrines, while the Celtic experience is that of a place authenticated locally because of its association with the actual earthly life of the saint. If we are to understand these Celtic saints aright, and enjoy them, which is perhaps even more important, our starting point must be to set them in this context of the strong sense of family. I am made aware once again of that very strong corporate sense of Celtic Christianity.[1] Kin-love is a wonderful word which Blathmac, himself of course a monk, and a member of the monastic family, uses to describe Christ's love: "Your fair renowned Son, O Mary, was warm in kin-love." For kinship, the sense of belonging, was extraordinarily strong in these early years in Ireland and Wales. "Society was tribal, rural, hierarchical, and familiar" in the words of one historian, and that sense of kinship was one of the strongest organizing principles of early Celtic society.[2] The primary family group comprised all those related to one another in

162

the male line up to the second cousin: a number of such family groups made up the *tuath:* (there were about a hundred *tuatha* when St. Patrick arrived in Ireland): from the seventh century the basic landholding and legal unit was the extended family, the *fine.* The earliest monastic communities in Ireland fitted easily into this pattern. The only model available in countries that lacked any urban organization was the ring-fort of the small local king. Here were a succession of concentric circles at whose heart lay the immediate monastic family itself, the abbot and the brothers, the abbess and the sisters. The family then chooses its friends, tenants, artisans, servants, and other secular and lay people, who live within its orbit, men and women of varying social status who provide different services, in labor or rent, and whose aim and purpose in life is to support the monks and nuns and in turn be supported by them.

The monastery was therefore a huge complex, the focus for a network of interdependent and interconnected people. A big monastery in ninth-century Wales or Ireland would in effect be a township and college as well as religious center, a place of endless coming and going, in which small children were fostered and educated, learning pursued, manual work and skilled arts and craftsmanship practiced. All this took place under the leadership of an abbot or abbess who was himself or herself lay—which, as a leading Celtic historian reminds us, does not mean lowering of standards or secularization.[3] But the real center lay in the relics of the founding saint. The monks and nuns saw themselves as disciples of the saints. The monastery therefore looked inward to the saints and outward to the world around.

But ultimately it was the presence of the saint, the holy man and woman, that drew people, and gave to the place its real raison d'être. Celtic saints are tenaciously native and local. They have, from the beginning, been a natural part of life, associated above all with the place in which they lived out their vocation. The waters of the holy well after all are the very selfsame waters that they were in the lifetime of the saint. Men and women were deemed saints because of the memory of their lives of holiness (in many cases secret, almost hidden lives, particularly those less well known Welsh saints), rather than because of a decision by a remote ecclesiastical authority. By the late eighth century the Irish were very conscious of their saints and were drawing up lists of them. The earliest major text, *Martyrology of Tallaght*, the work of Oengus the Culdee at the end of the eighth century, had literally hundreds of Irish saints, over two hundred for January alone, suggesting that the compiler had consulted records and found lists of abbots, abbesses, and others whom the local churches remembered and prayed for. There are saints for every month and every season. In a prayer to the saints who preside over the different seasons, Adomnan, abbot of Iona to whom it is attributed, mentions the calendar of Oengus in the sixth verse, comparing it rather unfavorably with his own work.

> *The saints of the four seasons,*
> *I long to pray to them,*
> *May they save me from torments,*
> *The saints of the whole year!*

The saints of the glorious springtime,
May they be with me
By the will
Of God's fosterling [i.e., Christ].

The saints of the dry summer,
About them is my poetic frenzy,
That I may come from this land
To Jesus, Son of Mary.

The saints of the winter I pray to,
May they be with me against the throng of demons,
Around Jesus of the mansions,
The Spirit Holy, heavenly.

The other calendar,
Which noble saints will have,
Though it has more verses,
It does not have more saints.

I beseech the saints of the earth,
I beseech all the angels,
I beseech God himself, both when rising and lying
     down,
Whatever I do or say, that I may dwell in the
     heavenly land.[4]

One of the most important seasonal celebrations of a saint
was that of St. Brigit (or Bride), whose feast day on Febru-

ary 1 seems to have incorporated pre-Christian elements into a Christian festival. This feast day comes at the end of the winter months, the three "dead" months of the year, when nature is asleep. Brigit, with her white wand, was said to breathe life into the mouth of the dead winter and bring him to open his eyes to the tears, the smiles, and laughter of spring. At the end of the last century in Scotland, Carmichael found this saying:

> *Bride put her finger in the river*
> *On the feast day of Bride*
> *And away went the hatching mother of the cold . . .*

But then a further connection was made with Candlemas, for it was said in Ireland that Bride walked before Mary with a lighted candle in each hand when she went up to the temple for purification, and although the winds were strong on the temple heights and the tapers were unprotected, they did not flicker or fail, and for this reason Bride is called "Bride of brightness."[5]

The calendar of Celtic saints records a saint on virtually every day of the year, with the feast days of the major saints quite naturally woven into the yearly pattern of life, and being the occasion for great celebrations. But in the Celtic countries the landscape itself has become virtually an ikonastasis, a living reminder of the presence of the saints. Celtic spirituality is above all a spirituality of place, and living as I do on the Welsh Borders, I cannot forget this. I am made aware of continuity, of the numbers of churches and wells commemorating the names of local saints, which have been there since the days of the saints themselves. For me one of the pleasures of discovering these Celtic saints has been that I have found so many humble men and women whose names would probably have been known only in their immediate neighborhood. Just as the oral tradition allows us to hear the voices of anonymous people who would otherwise be forgotten, so here we find the names of many who lived hidden, prayer-filled, apparently uneventful lives.

Place names in Wales very often begin with "Llan," meaning "clearing" or "open space" and which is then added to the name of the saint—and the many Llanfairs are the church of Mary. "Merthyr" means "memorial," a memorial to the saint. In Brittany "Loc" is frequently found as a prefix to a place name involving a Celtic saint, and "Kil" or "Cil" is found in Ireland or Scotland.[6] The unity of the Celtic world, the result of the comparative ease of sea travel, is reflected in the frequency with which names of the same saint occur in Wales and Ireland, Brittany and Cornwall as they moved so easily from one country to another. There may be a number of different places associated with different phases of the saint's life as he or she moved about. But in the midst of traveling and evangelizing, the deep yearning remained for withdrawal; the saints did not easily forget the pull of the desert. So there are also the remote places in which they set up a small oratory or cell where they will also be remembered, on mountaintops, in deep forested valleys, on desolate and stormy headlands, on small islands.

Few, if any, Celtic saints died by the sword, and there is not the same tradition of martyrdom here as there is in the

Roman calendar. Nevertheless, we should not underestimate the opposition they had to face and the serious difficulties and threats of those early years. We glimpse something of the obstacles to the propagation of the new faith in the *Letter to Coroticus,* that St. Patrick wrote to the Romano-British Christian ruler who had raided the Irish coast and killed and taken captive a group of recently baptized Christians. Noel Dermott O'Donoghue calls the letter "a sustained cry of anguish, almost a cry of despair," showing the suffering and anger of a man who has himself known what it is to be a slave and can therefore enter only too clearly into the degradation of his converts. St. Patrick calls Coroticus and his followers "rebels against Christ who will be scattered like clouds of smoke in the wind," their lot "the lake of everlasting fire."[7] Powerful and oppressive local rulers must have looked with fear on the progress of these saints invading their territories, men and women whose peaceful presence was such a threat to their power and authority. The Druids had been right in recognizing that when St. Patrick lighted the paschal fire those were flames that promised the ascendancy of Christ over their territories, and doubtless that had encouraged the high-king to try to kill him and his followers. So the saints lived with conflict and turmoil, but time and again, as in this case, their holiness will be demonstrated by the miraculous power of God at work in their lives.

We come to know their extraordinary stories through their *Lives.* The *Lives of the Saints* enjoy a unique status in early Celtic literature, neither history nor romance nor, strictly speaking, biography. The custom of writing the lives of the saints began, as in the monasteries of the East and Europe, because of the desire to preserve the memory of the founders and to hold the example of their holy lives up to the community. On the whole they were written several centuries later, though there are two that are rather exceptional in being written comparatively recently after the lifetime of the saint: Cogitosus's life of Brigid, the foundress of the monastery at Kildare in the late fifth or early sixth century, was written in the seventh century and is the earliest life of any Irish saint, and the life of St. Columba, who died in 597, was written by Adomnan, abbot of Iona, from 657 to 669. The immediate incentive for the writing of these *Lives* was almost certainly to promote the political interests of a particular church or monastic foundation and they must therefore be seen in the context of a concern to protect local rights and privileges. We owe the twelfth-century *Book of Llandaff,* for example, to the industry and devotion of Urban, Bishop of Llandaff, so that he could establish the rights of his new see to lands claimed by rivals in the dioceses of St. David's and Hereford, and because he felt himself threatened by the increasing interference of the Norman invaders. This is typical and it is vital to bear this in mind as we read these *Lives.*

Inevitably much of the writing will, therefore, be biased, even outrageous and bizarre, with accounts of miracles and miraculous happenings, impossible feats of endurance and improbable events, since as well as being prototypes for devotion, saints must also be shown to be persons who manifest power. So today we have to handle the *Lives* at many different levels: historical, mythical, psy-

chological, and, not least, spiritual. Many of their character-
istics are reminiscent of the native art of storytelling, and
the traditions of an aristocratic warrior society. We have
already seen the heroic nature of the Christ who is *Christus
Victor,* victorious after battle with the powers of darkness,
and nothing less is expected of the saints who follow him.
The *Lives* emphasize the heroic stature of the saint. There
are many similarities between saints and heroes; each essentially fighter, champion, victor. It is interesting to see how
parallel is the process of the making of a cult hero and of a
saint: both saints and heroes are named by popular voice,
elected to that status by a society that created them and
found in them an embodiment of their ideals and values.
The difference, as Peter Brown points out, is that while
heroes are mortals who earn their glory on earth and once
dead have no further connection with men and women, the
saints, in Christian belief, form a closer relationship with
God in death and are then able to intercede on behalf of
their fellow mortals when near the throne in heaven.[8]

If we try to root out tares from wheat in order to find
the truth buried in these lives, we shall only suffer frustration. They are essentially lives of miracle, a miraculous element that is there from the moment of birth, or even before. There are signs and wonders, with frequent symbolic
reference to light in many forms, for example, a shining
jewel. Among the stories of the birth of a saint, the birth of
St. Hilda, as told by Bede, is particularly vivid. St. Hilda's
mother, a member of an aristocratic family taking refuge
with a Celtic lord, had a dream in which she was seeking for
her husband (who was in fact shortly to be poisoned) and

instead discovered under her clothes a precious necklace. As she looked at it closely it emitted such a brilliant light that all Britain was lit by its splendor. This was, of course, the foreshadowing of the birth of that child with whom she was then pregnant, who was to illuminate the land in her lifetime, and bring light to pagan darkness and to the Church of her day. On the night of the birth of St. Brendan (whose mother, incidentally, had before his birth dreamed that her bosom was full of pure gold) the local Bishop Erc saw "all in one great blaze, and an attendance of angels in shining white garments all round that land." The rest of the life often follows a common pattern: the child, whose promise has been so clearly revealed, is given to the care, or fostering, of some good and learned man or woman, just as in secular society the practice of fostering was so common (the reflection of the role of the extended family) that Christ himself was described in the poem quoted above as God's "fosterling." At the age of two, St. Brendan was given to a nun, St. Ita, to foster, and he remained with her for five years, learning the rudiments of the dedicated life, doubtless with great gentleness and warmth, for to her is attributed the poem describing how the child Jesus comes to sleep on her bosom: "I will take nothing from my Lord," said she, "unless He gives me His Son from Heaven in the form of a baby to be nursed by me." So that Christ came to her in the form of a baby, and she said then:

Little Jesus, Who is nursed by me in my little hermitage—even a priest with store of wealth, all is false but little Jesus.

The nursing which I nurse in my house is not the nursing of any base churl, Jesus with the folk of Heaven at my heart every single night.[9]

Years of wandering and searching follow, perhaps traveling from one monastery to another seeking "the place of one's resurrection." In addition, there might also be times of solitude, living as a hermit in preparation for the life that lies ahead. Then comes the search for the right site, the building of the monastery, the arrival of the disciples, when the saints finally find the place that will hereafter bear their name, in which they will be father or mother, guide and counselor, to unnumbered souls in their own lifetime, and beyond. The origin of the monastery of Clonmacnois was foretold in a vision in which St. Enda, the master, and St. Ciaran, the novice, on the island of Aranmore, both saw a great and fruitful tree spreading its shade from the bank of the river Shannon over all the parts of Ireland, from its inner country to the coast. When St. Ciaran asked what this might mean, his master replied, "My son, that tree is you yourself; for your renown will fill Ireland, and the grace of God in you will avail for its people far and wide," referring to the role that the monastery would play in the future of the Church.

The *Lives* make excellent reading, full of encounters with enemies, friends, angels, the wild creatures, the elements themselves, all of which encourages vivid storytelling. One of the most delightful stories is that of St. Brigid and the sunbeam, given here in the original seventh-century version of Cogitosus's *Life.*

It happened that she was pasturing her sheep on a grassy spot on the plain when she was soaked by heavy rain, and she returned home in wet clothes. The sun shining through a gap in the building cast a ray which, at first glance, seemed to her to be a solid wooden beam fixed across the house. She placed her wet cloak upon it as if it were indeed solid, and the cloak hung securely from the incorporeal sunbeam. When the inhabitants of the house spread the word of this great miracle among the neighbours, they extolled the incomparable Brigid with fitting praise . . .[10]

We see how the natural elements respond to the holiness of the saint in the *Life* of St. Ninian when for a moment that blessed sanctity breaks down.

Whenever he rested from his journey, either for his own sake or for that of the animal he rode, he took out a book which he carried for the very purpose . . . the divine power granted him such grace that even when resting in the open air, when reading in the heaviest rain, no dampness ever touched the book upon which his mind was concentrated. When everything around him was soaked, he sat alone with his little book in the downpour, as if protected by the roof of a house.

But once, taking out his Psalter as usual:

the light air, like a room surrounding the servants of God, resisted the downpour like an impenetrable wall.

But as they sang, the most blessed Ninian took his eyes from the book as an unlawful thought stirred in him and desire prompted by the devil. Immediately the rain fell upon him and his book . . . .[11]

The miraculous is ever present and the raising of the dead to life is almost a staple diet of the *Lives*. One story will do for all the rest. It is told about St. Padarn, a sixth-century saint, when his great foundation in Ceredigion was later trying to promote its interests (in the early twelfth century) that when the saint heard that one of his servants had been killed by thieves while he was in the woods of the monastery, he set off calling the servant by name. " 'Reply, Reaus, to thy master.' The head, torn from the corpse, replied, 'Here I be, sir.' With which word the bishop came up to the place whence had come the reply, and, seeing the head separated from the body, with eyes lifted to heaven he blessed the whole corpse, whereupon head and body were conjointed and the servant rose alive, and both gave thanks for Christ's miracle."[12]

Yet while at one moment the saints may be making miraculous cures or achieving impossible tasks, the next moment they will be performing kind, gentle, humble actions which bring their lives into touch with the lives of ordinary men and women. This is particularly true of St. Brigit, who was very close to women because of the way in which she acted as midwife or aid-woman at the birth of Christ. Her story was presented in terms that would be familiar to the hearers: She is the serving maid in the inn at Bethlehem when two strangers come to the door. "The man was old, with brown hair and grey beard, and the woman was young and beautiful. She could not give them shelter but she did give them of her own bannock and stoup of water, and her heart was sore that she could not do more for them." Later on she saw a brilliant golden light over the stable door, and was in time to aid and minister Mary at the birth and receive the Child into her arms. The legend continues with a wonderful lack of any sense of linear time: "When the Child was born, Bride put three drops of water from the spring of pure water on His forehead, in name of God, in name of Jesus, in name of Spirit." In consequence she is known as the aid-woman of Mary and when a woman is in labor the midwife will go to the door of the house and stand on the doorstep with her hands on the jamb, beseeching Brigit to come: "Bride! Bride! come in, Thy welcome is truly made."[13]

There are so many wonderful stories of the mutual respect and service between the saints and the wild creatures that it becomes almost impossible to know how to select from the numbers of delightful examples of these mutual friendships. When Mo Chua, who was a contemporary of St. Columba's, lived in his hermitage in the wilderness:

He had no worldly wealth but a cock and a mouse and a fly. The work the cock used to do for him was to keep matins at midnight. Now, the mouse would not allow him to sleep more than five hours in a day and a night; and when he wished to sleep longer, being tired from much cross-vigil and prostration, the mouse would begin nibbling his ear, and so awoke him. Then the fly, the work it did was to walk along every line he read in his Psalter, and when he rested from singing his Psalms the fly would stay on the line he had left until he returned again to read his Psalms.[14]

St. Ciaran of Saighir had in his household a wild boar, a deer, a badger, and a fox,

> who remained with him in the greatest docility, for they obeyed the orders of the holy man in everything like monks. One day, however, the Fox grew tired of the vegetarian regime and stole his master's shoes and went off to his old den, intending to devour them there. Learning this, the holy father Ciaran sent another monk, or pupil, namely the Badger, to the wilderness after the Fox to bring back the brother to his place. And the Badger, who was well acquainted with the woods, obeying at once the word of his superior, set out and came straight to the cave of brother Fox; and when he found him about to devour the shoes of his master, he cut off his ears and tail and plucked out his hairs and compelled him to come with him to the monastery to do penance for his theft. And the Fox, compelled perforce, came along with the Badger to St. Ciaran in his cell at nones, bringing the shoes unharmed. And the holy man said to the Fox, "Why have you done this sin, brother, which monks ought not to do? Behold, our water is pure and common to all, and the food likewise is apportioned to all in common; and if you had desired to eat flesh according to your in-

stinct, almighty God would have made it for you from the bark of trees." Then the Fox, begging for forgiveness, did penance by fasting and did not touch food until the holy man commanded it. Thereupon he remained in the fellowship of the others.[15]

There were many useful tasks that the creatures performed for those saints who were scribes and scholars. A bird drops a feather to make a pen for St. Molass of Devenish when he needs one; a stag rests a book on its antlers so that St. Cainnech of Aghaboe can study while he walks in the forest; a fox who is a friend of St. Ciaran of Clonmacnois becomes the go-between for him and his tutor, "humbly attending the lesson until the writing of it on wax came to an end and then he would take it with him to Ciaran."

Friendship with the angels, which means comfortable companionship and familiar converse, played an important part in the saints' lives. It is the most matter-of-fact thing recorded by St. David's biographer, "After Matins he proceeded alone to hold converse with the angels." His monks called him "an associate of angels." At the time of St. Brendan's death St. Columba said, "In this past night I have seen the sky suddenly opened, and companies of angels coming down to meet the soul of St. Brendan. Their shining and incomparable brightness in that hour lit up the whole circle of the world." As death approaches, the presence of the angels becomes an essential part of the death scene, a return to the theme of light found at the birth of the saint. The description of the death of St. Columba shows most clearly how the saint, who has walked with the angels in his life (on Iona one can still see the "hill of the angels," where "from time to time the citizens of heaven used to be seen coming down to converse with the saint"), comes even closer to them as death approaches. On the Sabbath, the day before the day of his death, the monks see him "with his eyes gazing upwards, looked suffused with a ruddy bloom" the reason being that he alone had seen an angel flying above him, actually in the church, sent "to recover a loan dear to God," which of course refers to his own soul. He blesses the island, he bids farewell to the weeping horse, sits in his hut copying the Psalms, and then finally goes to bed after vespers. At midnight, on the sound of the bell, he got up for the midnight office and running in ahead of the others knelt alone in prayer before the altar. "In the same instant his servant Diarmait following behind saw from a distance the whole church filled inside with angelic light around the saint," and going in found him lying in front of the altar, his face still "ruddy with the joy of seeing an angel so that it seemed to belong to a living sleeper, not to a dead man." At the same time another saint in Ireland had a vision of Iona bathed in the bright light of angels. "And all the air and sky above even to the heavenly ether was filled with the radiance of the countless angels sent down from heaven to carry home his soul. I heard the most sweet songs of the angelic hosts singing on high in the very moment when his soul departed and was carried up among the choirs of angels."[16]

It is because the saints are bringers of light, as their

birth foretold, that underlying everything else I feel that we are being made aware of the battle of good and evil, of dark and light. We can still read these lives and find in them inspiration for our own lives in that same battle. That battle is nowhere more dramatically recounted than in the heroic journey of St. Brendan in *Navigatio Brendani,* or *Voyage of Brendan.*[17] Outwardly this is the story of a sea voyage, undertaken by St. Brendan the navigator (there are several other Irish saints called Brendan), who lived between 480 and 570, a monk and later abbot at Ardfert, who founded the monastery of Clonfert, where he is buried. He sets out on a journey that lasts seven years in search of a land promised to the saints, the Isles of the Blessed, paradise itself. In the 1970s Tim Severin set out to follow St. Brendan, making for himself a leather boat, based on the description given in the *Navigatio,* and in this fragile craft sailed with four companions from Ireland across the Atlantic, eventually reaching Newfoundland. To take the voyage as geographical exploration, however, is to see it as something that it was never intended to be. Instead, we should put it into the context of the voyage narratives known as *immrama,* a literary form full of vigor, imagination, larger-than-life heroes, popular in pre-Christian Ireland. This is both journey literature, humanity's search for the meaning of life, and vision literature, the universal quest for a happy "other-world," both as old as mankind. In the hands of the Irish storytellers there were endless adventures, in otherworldly landscapes with supernatural wonders, but always in the end the hero and his companions finally return home.[18]

An insatiable questing was part of the Celtic spirit, a longing to see what lay over the horizon, for living close to the sea affects the senses. Adomnan gives a vivid picture of a people who appear nearly amphibious, always coming out of a boat or seeking one, a life where the blowing of the wind in a sail, the loathsome and dangerous creatures of the ocean, were everyday realities. But it was not simply the physical presence of the sea. The sea is a place of liminality, a boundary, a frontier, between two places, and if the search is for the meaning of life, what better place in which to site it? So the sea also becomes a place of revelation, a source of wisdom, a medium through which messages come from the "other-world."

The *Navigatio* opens with a monk called Barinthus telling St. Brendan of his discovery of an island of delights where "there is no obscuring darkness but only perpetual day." St. Brendan resolves to see this for himself, and after prayer and fasting, with fourteen carefully chosen companions, he sets out on his own journey, seven years of voyaging. The *Navigatio* is the account of the extraordinary mysteries, delights, horrors, monstrosities that he encounters as the boundary between the natural and the supernatural fades away. They are warmly received by a succession of different monastic communities:

> Brothers came from their various cells like bees to meet us. Their dwelling places were scattered but still they lived together in faith, hope, and love, with one refectory, and they always gathered for the divine office.

They were served no food other than fruits, nuts, roots, and other kinds of vegetables. And after Compline, each remained in his own cell until cockcrow or the ringing of a bell.

I love this gentle picture of a Celtic monastic city. On another island they find St. Ailbe with his community of silent contemplative monks, St. Ailbe himself being a contemporary of St. Patrick's, for here time is not chronological time but a *kairos* time of symbolically significant events. Later, on another island, they meet another contemporary of St. Patrick's, a solitary who greets them with the psalmist's words "Behold, how good and joyful thing it is for brethren to dwell together in unity."

There are endless perils and glories: They sail through pillars of crystal, they meet with monsters, they land on an island which then heaves and turns into a whale, they stay on the island of birds who join in the offices with them. At one point, when his monks are terrified by the creatures of the deep who surround their boat, St. Brendan sturdily says, "How can you be afraid of them? Is not our Lord Jesus Christ the Lord of Creation?" These seven years bring them the chance to witness the mysteries of creation, and to reflect on the presence of the creator in the phenomenon of creation. We are reminded of what St. Columbanus said, "Understand creation if you would understand the Creator." When a monster is pursuing them, St. Brendan asks the brethren: "Do you see, dear monks, the marvels of the Lord, and the obedience which the creature renders to the

Creator?" There is wonder, deep interest in the natural world, a mystical vision of creation which sees the whole of creation open to the redeeming grace of God.

But there is another level on which to understand the *Navigatio*. It is also about conflict, set within the popular form of a journey or pilgrimage that involves spiritual or psychological struggle. It is an internal journey; it is a battlefield within himself. St. Brendan is a man of God engaged in battle and his fellow monks are fellow warriors. That it is a tale about monks by monks was something that Thomas Merton recognized at once when he wrote in his journal for July 18, 1964: "I began it this morning studying it as a tract on monastic life. The myth of pilgrimage: the quest for the impossible island, the earthly paradise, the ultimate ideal."[19] For it is above all liturgical prayer and liturgical time that provide the structure of the journey as it unfolds around the two key anchor points, the Easter cycle spent in the environs of the island of sheep, and the Christmas cycle with the monastic community of Ailbe. This is no linear journey: All the times are significant numbers: forty, three, seven. It is a seven-year journey, and when they finally reach the promised land, St. Brendan and his monks spend forty days there and then return home. They stay for three days on various islands, they pray and fast for three days, the wind ceases after three days. The whole thing is set outside time and space. We are watching the interplay between the temporal and the eternal, the times and places of this world and the divine reality that infuses them. The question the *Navigatio* raises is: "How does one live out of a transfigured center?" The saints knew that human time is contained within, and unfolds within, the dimension of the eternal.

St. Brendan, this *vir Dei*, "man of God," engaged in battle, is a hero who, when he dies will be welcomed into the company of heaven, and will join all those who, like him, have done battle, suffered, and won. The *Martyrology of Tallaght* gives a picture of a king welcoming men and women into his kingdom, those kingfolk whom the poet longs to join: "May I be for ever with thy kingfolk, in thy eternal, glorious Kingdom."

For this is the promise held out to all who follow the saints:

> *It were my mind's desire to behold the face of God.*
> *It were my mind's desire to be for ever in the*
>   *company of the King.*

The writing tells us much about how people felt about their saints around the shining throne of God, who is addressed as "the sun." In the epilogue we see all these kingfolk gathered up like "troops with noble overkings, a bright white following, the vast host of saints," and the final words are:

> *I have commemorated the kingfolk around the King,*
>   *above the clouds.*
> *O bright Sun that illuminest heaven with much of*
>   *holiness! O King that rulest angels, O Lord of*
>   *men!*
> *O Lord of men, O King righteous, truly good, let*
>   *every profit be mine for my praise of thy kingfolk.*

Thy kingfolk whom I praise . . . The fair people
with beauty, the kingfolk I have commemorated.[20]

Here is the family of heaven around the throne facing God, their delight to gaze on him. "The saints have need of nothing but to be listening to the music to which they listen and to look on the light which they see, and to be filled with the fragrance which is in the land"—in the words of an anonymous eleventh-century Irish writer.[21]

This household of heaven, God's royal hall, is a merry company. Did the Irish perhaps keep at the back of their minds the memory of the color and music of the great halls of Tara, the traditional gathering place of the high-king with its twelve couches for his followers? And, just as the high-king reigned from that low hill so he was never seen to be far distant from his people, so also was heaven felt to be close to earth. That is why an old woman in the southwest of Ireland today can think of inviting the whole company of heaven into her cottage. She feels at home with God and his saints, and shows them the same hospitality that she would to any of her neighbors.

> *I would like to have the men of Heaven*
> *In my own house:*
> *With vats of good cheer*
> *Laid out for them . . .*
>
> *I would like a great lake of beer*
> *For the King of Kings,*

I would like to be watching Heaven's family
Drinking it through all eternity.[22]

The Celtic sense of the communion of saints comes across
very strongly in a poem by Gwenallt in which he says that
the barriers go down between this world and the next, and
St. David comes among us in Wales today, traveling around
the country like a gypsy, going into schools and colleges,
mines and factories, and finally coming into our own
homes:

There is no barrier between two worlds in the
    Church,
The Church militant on earth
Is one with the Church triumphant in heaven,
And the saints are in this church which is two
    in one.
They come to worship with us, our small
    congregation,
The saints our oldest ancestors . . .

He carried the Church everywhere
Like a body with life and mind and will,
And he did things small and great.
He brought the Church into our homes,
Put the holy vessels on the kitchen table
With bread from the pantry and wine from the
    cellar,
And he stood behind the table like a tramp
So as not to hide from us the wonder of the sacrifice.

*And after the Communion we had a talk round the
fire
And he spoke to us of God's natural order . . .*[23]

The Celtic saints remind us that we are "keeping house amidst a cloud of witnesses." We in our own day, going about our daily tasks, are yet surrounded in our nice little safe and ordinary households by that greater household and company, the company of the kingfolk of heaven.

10

PRAISE

SO THE CELTIC vision of the end of time is a splendid one: the expectation that in the next world we shall all join the saints and the whole household of heaven, a merry company rejoicing around the throne of God. Since poetry and music came so naturally to them, it was hardly surprising that Celtic people should expect to be "listening to the music to which they listen." Their natural capacity for rejoicing means that praise, celebration, thanksgiving, are the foundation of their life of prayer. Their one desire, expressed in this twelfth-century Irish poem, is to praise God in perfect form:

> *My speech—may it praise you without flaw: may my heart love you, King of Heaven and of earth.*

> *My speech—may it praise you without flaw: make it easy for me, great Lord, to do you all service and to adore you.*

> *My speech—may it praise you without flaw: Father of all affection hear my poems and my speech.*[1]

The line that comes again and again in another twelfth-century poem is "unfaltering praise of mine!"

Lord, be it thine,
Unfaltering praise of mine!
To thee my whole heart's love be given
Of earth and Heaven Thou King divine!

Lord, be it thine,
Unfaltering praise of mine!
And, O pure prince! make clear my way
To serve and pray at thy sole shrine!

Lord, be it thine,
Unfaltering praise of mine!
O father of souls that long,
Take this my song and make it thine![2]

One of the earliest surviving written examples of Welsh poetry catches the mood of *gorfoleddu*, "ecstatic rejoicing," exuberance, exultant praise of the creator who saves the world that he has made:

Almighty creator, thou hast made the land and the
  sea . . .

The world cannot express in song bright and
  melodious, even though the grass and the trees
  should sing, all thy glories [miracles, riches] O
  true Lord!

The Father has wrought such a multitude of wonders
  in this world that it is difficult to find an equal

number. Letters cannot contain it, letters cannot
express it.

Jesus wrought on behalf of the hosts of Christendom
such a multitude of miracles when he came, like
grass is the number of them.

He who made the wonder of the world, will save us,
has saved us. It is not too great toil to praise the
Trinity.[3]

This God is a God who saves. Even in the act of praising
creation God's redemptive work is not forgotten. Just as we
have seen in those long litanies that go on and on a pouring
out of the grief of the heart, so here do we find long poems
of rejoicing that go on and on a pouring out of praise.

In "The Loves of Taliesin," one of the greatest works of
medieval Welsh literature, we can see this holding together
particularly well. The theme of the poem is penance, the
desire for penance, and the opening words address the God
who saves, "Beautiful too that God shall save me" and "But
loveliest of all is covenant/With God on the Day of Judgment" are its closing words. But between them come this
cascading list of the glories of the created world, which
ranges over the social, the natural, the religious. It is rather
too long to quote in full. Here is the second half:

The beauty of summer, its days long and slow,
Beautiful too visiting the ones we love.
The beauty of flowers on the tops of fruit trees,

Beautiful too covenant with the Creator.
The beauty in the wilderness of doe and fawn,
Beautiful too the foam-mouthed and slender steed.
The beauty of the garden when the leeks grow well,
Beautiful too charlock in bloom.
The beauty of the horse in its leather halter,
Beautiful too keeping company with a king.
The beauty of a hero who does not shun injury,
Beautiful too is elegant Welsh.
The beauty of the heather when it turns purple,
Beautiful too moorland for cattle.
The beauty of the season when calves suckle,
Beautiful too riding a foam-mouthed horse.
And for me there is no less beauty
In the father of the horn in a feast of mead.
The beauty of the fish in his bright lake,
Beautiful too its surface shimmering.
The beauty of the word which the Trinity speaks,
Beautiful too doing penance for sin.
But the loveliest of all is covenant
With God on the Day of Judgement.[4]

"Glorious Lord I give you greeting!" One of the earliest of
the Welsh praise poems, dated to the tenth or eleventh century, starts with this salutation to God. It is in the direct
manner of the psalmist and in its use of short lines with two
stresses has something of the same ejaculatory quality found
in the Benedicite or Psalm 148. Patrick Thomas calls it "this
beautiful Celtic Benedicite, with its praise tumbling forth in

an ecstatic appreciation of God's all-embracing glory."[5] All things offer praise to God, human and cosmic and religious brought together into one dynamic web of interconnectedness. A sense of spiraling circularity is deepened by the way in which the first and last lines echo each other. The whole feeling of the poem is that of the unity of the universe and how we ourselves are caught up into that unity:

> *Glorious Lord, I give you greeting!*
> *Let the church and the chancel praise you.*
> *Let the chancel and the church praise you.*
> *Let the plain and the hillside praise you.*
> *Let the world's three well-springs praise you.*
> *Two above wind and one above land.*
> *Let the dark and the daylight praise you.*
> *Abraham, founder of the faith, praised you:*
> *Let the life everlasting praise you.*
> *Let the birds and the honeybees praise you.*
> *Let the shorn stems and the shoots praise you.*
> *Both Aaron and Moses praised you:*
> *Let the male and the female praise you.*
> *Let the seven days and the stars praise you.*
> *Let the air and the ether praise you.*
> *Let the books and the letters praise you.*
> *Let the fish in the swift streams praise you.*
> *Let the thought and the action praise you.*
> *Let the sand-grains and the earth-clods praise you.*
> *And I shall praise you, Lord of glory:*
> *Glorious Lord, I give you greeting!*[6]

Church and the chancel are images that represent the dimension of grace; mountains and hills that of nature—clearly the natural world that the poet himself knows, not some idealized world, for how otherwise would he include the stubble and the grass? The three fountains are the sun, the moon, and saltwater of Celtic cosmology, so again an incorporation of pre-Christian thought. Abraham, Aaron, and Moses represent biblical faith, and "life everlasting" is the promise of Christianity. Male and female speak of the totality of the human person, books and letters, thought and action, the dimensions of the intellect and the imagination. When at the end comes the voice of the poet, that can also be my voice. In a subtle way it is the raising to God of the poet's voice, speaking praise on behalf of creation, that becomes the focus of the poem and makes it this creative act of praise, of the Pauline new creation itself, the breaking down of all the divides of time and place. So inner and outer, the gifts of creation and the gifts of redemption, the Old and the New Testaments, are all brought together into this glorious unity.

The praise poem, the cultic celebration of the pagan king by professional poets, is another pre-Christian form that was taken up and turned to new use for the Christian God. He is, after all, as we have seen, a God who saves his people, a hero, the warrior who has overcome the enemy forces and to whom praise is due from his people. Christ is depicted as a conquering hero in a text from tenth- or eleventh-century Wales that still quite consciously imitates the language of secular tradition, not least by the repeated use of words emphasizing the action and achievement the God who defends, liberates, brings salvation, and leads to the feast.

> *In the name of the Lord, mine to praise, of great*
>   *praise,*
> *I shall praise God, great the triumph of his love,*
> *God who defended us, God who made us, God who*
>   *saved us,*
> *God our hope, perfect and honourable, beautiful his*
>   *blessing.*
> *We are in God's power, God above, Trinity's king.*
> *God proved himself our liberation by his suffering,*
> *God came to be imprisoned in humility.*
> *Wise Lord, who will free us by Judgement Day,*
> *Who will lead us to the feast through his mercy and*
>   *sanctity*
> *In Paradise, in pure release from the burden of sin,*
> *Who will bring us salvation through penance and the*
>   *five wounds,*
> *Terrible grief, God defended us when he took on*
>   *flesh.*
> *Man would be lost if the perfect rite had not*
>   *redeemed him.*
> *Through the cross, blood-stained, came salvation to*
>   *the world.*
> *Christ, strong shepherd, his honour shall not fail.*[7]

The *Altus Prosator* attributed to St. Columba, one of the greatest of all Celtic hymns, celebrates creation, the fall, the last things: God is creator and judge. It has much about the destructive forces at work in the world, but there are also stanzas in which the whole creation is once more seen in that ordered harmony and goodness which the creator had intended:

The Most High, planning the frame and harmony of
* the world,*
had made heaven and earth, had fashioned the sea
* and the waters,*
and also shoots of grass, the little trees of the woods,
the sun, the moon and the stars, fire and necessary
* things,*
birds, fish and cattle, beasts and living creatures,
and finally the first-formed man, to rule with
* prophecy.*

At once, when the stars were made, lights of the
* firmament,*
the angels praised for His wonderful creating
the Lord of this immense mass, the Craftsman of the
* Heavens.*
With a praiseworthy proclamation, fitting and
* unchanging,*
in an excellent symphony they gave thanks to the
* Lord,*
not by any endowment of nature, but out of love
* and choice.*

The poem speaks of the Second Coming, "When Christ, the most high Lord, comes down from the heavens/the brightest sign and standard of the Cross will shine forth." And finally we are given a vision of the scene around the throne with the Trinity praised in endless and eternal song:

> *By the singing of hymns eagerly ringing out,*
> *by thousands of angels rejoicing in holy dances,*
> *and by the four living creatures full of eyes,*
> *with the twenty-four joyful elders*
> *casting their crowns under the feet of the Lamb of*
>   *God,*
> *the Trinity is praised in eternal threefold exchanges.*[8]

I have found this praise of creation, the praise that comes from relationship with the created world, very moving, for it so obviously comes out of knowledge and love. It shows gentle observation, with time and attention, mindfulness to changing seasons, to shadows of delicate coloring, to changes of shape and form. An eighteenth-century Welsh Methodist minister as he looks and listens to a bird exclaims, "You enrich and astound us." Here wonder turns to praise, to gratitude for this bird as the work of God:

> *Lowly bird, beautifully taught,*
> *You enrich and astound us,*
> *We wonder long at your song,*
> *Your artistry and your voice.*
> *In you I see, I believe,*
> *The clear and excellent work of God.*
> *Blessed and glorious is he,*
> *Who shows his virtue in the lowest kind.*

How many bright wonders (clear note of loveliness)
Does this world contain?
How many parts, how many mirrors of his finest
  work
Offer themselves a hundred times to our gaze?
For the book of his art is a speaking light
Of lines abundantly full,
And every day one chapter after another
Comes among us to teach us of him.[9]

"Absolute attention is prayer." When May Sarton quoted those words of Simone Weil in her journal, she went on to say: "I have used that sentence often in talking about poetry to students, to suggest that if one looks long enough at almost anything, looks with absolute attention at a flower, a stone, the bark of a tree, grass, snow, a cloud, something like revelation takes place. Something is 'given . . .' "[10] I find the same quality as this in a late-ninth- or early-tenth-century poem about the coming of May with its extraordinary awareness of light, and of the variety and range of color, of sound, of touch. The bright shaft shot into the world is a brilliant way of describing a sunbeam!

May Day, season surprising!
Splendid is colour then.
Blackbirds sing a full lay,
If there be a slender shaft of day.

The dust-coloured cuckoo calls aloud:
Welcome, splendid summer!

The bitter bad weather is past,
The boughs of the wood are a thicket.

Summer cuts the river down,
The swift herd of horses seeks the pool,
The long hair of the heather is outspread,
The soft white wild-cotton blows.

A wild longing is on you to race horses
The ranked host is ranged around;
A bright shaft has been shot into the land,
So that the water-flag is gold beneath it.[11]

"God has not forbidden us to love the world," Gwenallt
tells us in the opening lines of one of his finest sonnets, and
he concludes by speaking of the day of resurrection on
which the body will be restored to us so that we may "per-
ceive the glories of God with all our senses."

God has not forbidden us to love the world,
And to love it with all the naked senses together,
Every shape and colour, every voice and every sound,
There is a shudder in our blood when we see
The traces of his craftsman's hands upon the
    world . . .[12]

Euros Bowen is another modern Welsh religious poet who
like Gwenallt reminds us that word craft is the country's
most powerful art form, as he uses words sacramentally,
creatively. In *Gloria,* a resounding hymn of praise:

The whole world is full of glory:

Here is the glory of created things,
   The earth and the sky,
      the sun and the moon,
         the stars and the vast expanses:

Here is fellowship
   with all that was created,
      the air and the wind,
         cloud and rain,
            sunshine and snow:
All life like the bubbling of a flowing river
   and the dark currents of the depths of the sea
      is full of glory.
The white waves of the breath of peace
   on the mountains,
      and the light striding
         in the distances of the sea:

The explosion of the dawn wood-pigeons
   and the fire of the sunset doves,
      sheep and cattle at their grazing,
         the joy of countless creeping things
            as they blossom,
               spider and ant
                  of nimble disposition
                     proclaim the riches of goodness[13]

When he speaks of the fellowship with all that was created, Euros Bowen brings us back again to one of the recurrent themes of Celtic spirituality—its corporate sense. Here is a sense of unity with all creation, both human and nonhuman, that transcends time and space and brings the whole world together as participants in the singing of one great hymn of praise. The hermit who might seem to be most alone in his or her cell praying the canonical hours and singing the Psalms is least alone. As Kenneth Jackson said of the early Irish ascetic nature poetry:

> The woodland birds might sing to him around his cell, but through it all, rarely expressed, always implicit, is the understanding that the bird and hermit are joining together in an act of worship; to him the very existence of nature was a song of praise in which he himself took part by entering into harmony with nature . . . It was from this harmony with nature, this all-perceiving contemplation of it, that the Irish hermits reached to a more perfect unison with God.

> *The woodland thicket overtops me.*
> *the blackbird sings me a lay, praise I will not*
>   *conceal:*
> *above my lined little booklet*
> *the trilling of birds sings to me.*[14]

The sharing of praise by humans and birds is caught in this story collected by Marjory Kennedy-Fraser from the songs of the Hebrides which ends with the promise that "the song of the birds will be in thine own heart." It tells how in the hard winter frost, as the birds were dying, the parish clerk was walking along the road to keep himself warm when "he saw one like a monk standing on a hillock near the Church of St. Kenneth, with a flock of birds flying round him. 'Who are thou, stranger, and what is thine errand?' asked the clerk. 'I am he whose name is on yonder Church, and I am giving Communion to the birds before they die.' 'Please God, holy man, they shall not die. I myself will feed them.' 'And the song of the birds will be in thine own heart . . .' "

> *Halleluia Praise ye ever Him, Ho halovichall O,*
> *Halleluia Praise ye ever Him, Ho halovichall O,*
> *Sing the birds His praise-song heaven-ward,*
> *Halleluia, Halleluia, Ho halovichall O.*[15]

This is something a mother in the Outer Hebrides, the wife of a simple crofter at the end of the last century, understands and wants to share with her children. She tells them that each day must start with the human voice joining in the song of the birds, since in the whole created order, all the creatures of earth, ocean, and sky were giving glory to God, it was not right that human beings should remain dumb. So from Ireland, Scotland, Wales, from the literate and the illiterate, from the earliest to the present day, comes this same message: Join in the worship of the whole universe.

My mother taught us what we should ask for in the prayer, as she heard it from her own mother, and as she again heard it from the one who was before her. My mother would be asking us to sing our morning song to God down in the back-house, as Mary's lark was singing it up in the clouds, and as Christ's mavis was singing it yonder in the tree, giving glory to the God of the creatures for the repose of the night, for the light of the day, and for the joy of life. She would tell us that every creature on the earth here below and in the ocean beneath and in the air above was giving glory to the great God of the creatures and the worlds, of the virtues and the blessings, and would *we* be dumb![16]

The theme of the morning songs which Alexander Carmichael heard is always that of the praise and thanksgiving due to a God who has placed us in the world of his creating. The start of each day, therefore, becomes a great shout of praise:

> *Thanks to Thee, O God, that I have risen to-day,*
> > *To the rising of this life itself;*
> *May it be to Thine own glory, O God of every*
> > *gift . . .*[17]

> *Thanks to Thee ever, O gentle Christ,*
> > *That Thou hast raised me freely from the black*
> *And from the darkness of last night*
> > *To the kindly light of this day.*

Praise unto Thee, O God of all creatures,
　　According to each life Thou hast poured on me,
My desire, my word my sense, my repute,
　　My thought, my deed, my way, my fame.[18]

"O Lord and God of life," "O Father everlasting and God of life," "Father eternal and God of mankind"—these are the names by which God is addressed. He is seen above all as the source and giver of life. One long creation credal celebration has this almost litanylike quality about it. Alexander Carmichael heard it from Mary Gillies, whom he described as "tall, erect, and stately. Her face was oval, her features fine, and her brown hair abundant. She sang this poem in a recitative voice." When people talked freely to him, and in their own way, he found that "music and poetry and pleasure flow back, and all rejoice."

I believe, O God of all gods,
　　That Thou art the eternal Father of life;
I believe, O God of all gods,
　　That Thou art the eternal Father of love.

I believe, O God of all gods,
　　That Thou art the eternal Father of the saints;
I believe, O God of all gods,
　　That Thou art the eternal Father of each one.

I believe, O God of all gods,
　　That Thou art the eternal Father of mankind;

I believe, O God of all gods,
  That Thou art the eternal Father of the world.

I believe, O Lord and God of the peoples,
That Thou art the creator of the high heavens,
That Thou art the creator of the skies above,
That Thou art the creator of the oceans below.

I believe, O Lord and God of the peoples,
  That Thou art He Who created my soul and set
    its warp,

Who created my body from dust and from ashes,
  Who gave to my body breath, and to my soul its
    possession . . .

Thanks be to Thee, Jesu Christ,
  For the many gifts Thou hast bestowed on me,
Each day and night, each sea and land,
  Each weather fair, each calm, each wild.

I am giving Thee worship with my whole life,
  I am giving Thee assent with my whole power,
I am giving Thee praise with my whole tongue,
  I am giving Thee honour with my whole
    utterance.

I am giving Thee reverence with my whole
  understanding,
    I am giving Thee offering with my whole
      thought,

I am giving Thee praise with my whole fervour,
   I am giving Thee humility in the blood of the
      Lamb.

I am giving Thee love with my whole devotion,
   I am giving Thee kneeling with my whole desire,
I am giving Thee love with my whole heart,
   I am giving Thee affection with my whole sense;
I am giving Thee existence with my whole mind,
   I am giving Thee my soul, O God of all gods.[19]

When life is seen as the gift of God, praise and thanks-giving are inevitable. When reverence and respect for the material world, for the earth itself, for the mundane activi-ties of daily work, are a natural part of life, then there can never be any denigration of matter itself. The generosity of God in sharing the goodness of creation with us can elicit only one possible response—that of gratitude. But gratitude is an activity that requires active participation on our part if it is to become central in our lives. Often praise does not rise naturally and easily to my lips! I have to confess that quite often it is hard work, needing to be renewed and sustained, for I tend to drift without noticing good gifts. One small phrase in these morning prayers which I love is "gently and generously" when describing the mercies which God has showered upon us:

Pray I this day my prayer to Thee, O God,
Voice I this day as voices the voice of Thy mouth,

Keep I this day as keep the people of heaven,
Spend I this day as spend Thine own household . . .

Each day may I remember the sources of the mercies
  Thou hast bestowed on me gently and
    generously;
Each day may I be fuller in love to Thyself
                  . . . .

Each thing I have received from Thee it came,
Each thing for which I hope, from Thy love it will
  come,
Each thing I enjoy, it is of Thy bounty,
Each thing I ask, comes of Thy disposing.

Holy God, loving Father, of the word everlasting,
Grant me to have of Thee this living prayer:
Lighten my understanding, kindle my will, begin my
  doing,
Incite my love, strengthen my weakness, enfold my
  desire . . .

And grant Thou to me, Father beloved,
From Whom each thing that is freely flows,
That no tie over-strict, no tie over-dear
  May be between myself and this world below.[20]

The line of this prayer which asks that there may be "no tie over-strict, no tie over-dear" between myself and the things below is a reminder that detachment, or non-attachment, is a vital element in praise. As soon as I start to possess, to control, or to organize, I cannot be open to the receiving of God's gifts with the freedom that they demand. I want to be able to look with gentleness, taking time to allow each thing to reach me with its own voice. So ultimately I cannot praise without being changed. As David Jones puts it, "If poetry is praise, as prayer is, it can never coexist with any malignant and persistent criticism of the nature of things."[21]

Celtic praise is shared praise, shared with the whole created world, human and nonhuman alike. Again I am brought back to the formative influence of the monastic tradition since a monastic choir praises God in harmony. "A conversation-in-song between brethren expresses a confidence in the presence of God in the presence of people to each other," as the editors of the early monastic poetry of Iona put it:

> Let us sing every day
> harmonising in turns,
> together proclaiming to God
> a hymn worthy of holy Mary.
>
> In two-fold chorus, from side to side,
> let us praise Mary,
> so that the voice strikes every ear
> with alternating praise.[22]

This is a whole hymn addressed to Mary by a chorus of singers who seem to be saying "Let us sing!" "Let us praise Mary!" as an act of shared celebration together. Here we have a body of people who pray, as it were, by mutual exhortation, joining in this choral recitation, so that prayer and praise are enhanced by shared communion.

In the Psalms this shared praise is expressed par excellence. If we are to appreciate the Celtic way of prayer, we must turn to the Psalms themselves. For monastic life, in the Celtic tradition as elsewhere, was shaped by the daily, weekly, yearly recitation of the Psalms, and in particular by the daily saying of Psalms 148 to 150, Psalms of praise. The Psalter was the prayer book that shaped their lives, shaped the way in which they saw God. It was from the Latin Psalter that a child would first learn to read at the age of seven. And then Adomnan's *Life of St. Columba* tells us that on the very last day of the saint's life:

> When he had come down from the hill and returned to the monastery, he sat in his cell writing out a copy of the Psalms. As he reached that verse of the thirty-fourth Psalm, where it is written, "They that seek the Lord shall not want for anything that is good," he said: "Here at the end of the page I must stop. Let Baithene write what follows." . . . When the saint had finished his verse at the bottom of the page, he went to the church for vespers on the night before Sunday.[23]

So from the start of life until its end the Psalms became an integral part of their lives. When the scholar monk, Mael Isu Ua Brollchain (who died in 1086) chanced on the old and tattered copy of the Psalter with which he had learned to read at the age of seven, he addressed it as *"Crinoc,"* "dear little thing." He wrote a love poem to her, remembering how "we slept, we two, as man and womankind," and describing the relationship as the best of loves:

Crinoc, lady of measured melody,
　　not young, but with modest maiden mind,
together once in Niall's northern land,
　　we slept, we two, as man and womankind.

You came and slept with me for that first time,
　　skilled wise amazon annihilating fears,
and I a fresh-faced boy, not bent as now,
　　a gentle lad of seven melodious years.

Your counsel is ever there to hand,
　　we choose it, following you in everything,
love of your word is the best of loves,
　　our gentle conversation with the king.

Seeking the presence of elusive God
　　wandering we stray, but the way if found,
following the mighty melodies that with you
　　throughout the pathways of the world resound.

Not ever silent, you bring the word of God
　　to all who in the present world abide,
and then through you the finest mesh,
　　man's earnest prayer to God is purified.[24]

This poem seems quite clearly to speak of the Psalms as melodies. Once we are told of the Psalter being sung antiphonally on a journey with a chant so sweet that St. Mochuta was spellbound by the sound, and thought that never had he heard such sweet singing. On another occasion we learn how the three young clerics who go out fishing said the daily office as they fished, "euphonic readings" as a twelfth-century composition described them. These are only occasional glimpses, but they suggest the extent to which the Psalms were so totally interwoven into their lives.[25] Prayer-headings were used for each Psalm in order to keep the presence of Christ before them as they prayed, a practice that spread from Ireland to become popular in Europe. Perhaps like Anskar, the ninth-century Frankish saint, they also wrote a brief prayer to say at the ending of each one. He called it a pigment, the essence of the color, the gathering of the flavor of each psalm.[26]

They knew the Psalms by heart, part of their liturgical lives and their personal prayer. Henri Nouwen found what this can mean after his experience of living and praying for several months in a Trappist monastery in America. He said that the Psalms of Compline:

> slowly become flesh in me . . . slowly these words enter into the center of my heart. They are more than ideas, images, comparison: they become a real presence . . . Many times I have thought if I am ever sent to prison, if I am ever subjected to hunger, pain, torture, or humiliation, I hope and pray that they let me keep the Psalms . . . How happy are those who no longer

need books but carry the Psalms in their heart wherever they are and wherever they go. Maybe I should
start learning the Psalms by heart so that nobody can
take them away from me.[27]

Thomas Merton, living the monastic life in the twentieth
century, has called the Psalms "at once the simplest and the
greatest of all religious poems. In the Psalms we drink divine praise at its pure and stainless source, in all its primitive sincerity and perfection. We return to the youthful
strength and directness with which the ancient psalmists
voiced their adoration of the God of Israel." He cannot
write of them except in the context of praise. He sees them
as the best possible way of praising God. "If we have no real
interest in praising Him it shows that we have never realized
who He is. For when one becomes conscious of who God
really is, and when one realizes that He who is Almighty,
and infinitely Holy, has done great things to us, the only
possible reaction is the cry of half-articulated exultation
that bursts from the depths of our being in amazement at
the tremendous, inexplicable goodness of God to men and
women."[28]

A ninth-century Irish hymn of praise takes up the dox-
ology found in Revelation 7:12, where we are told that the
angels who surround the throne of God worship him singing, "Praise and glory and wisdom, thanksgiving and
honor, power and might, be to our God forever and ever."

Blessing and brightness,
Wisdom, thanksgiving,

Great power and might
To the King who rules over all.

Glory and honour and goodwill,
Praise and the sublime song of minstrels,
Overflowing love from every heart
To the King of Heaven and Earth.

To the chosen Trinity has been joined
Before all, after all, universal
Blessing and everlasting blessing,
Blessing everlasting and blessing.[29]

Blessings have run throughout this book. As I come to its end, I realize that it is only now, in the context of praise, that I can fully realize what Celtic blessings are about. They do not beg or ask God to give this or that. Instead, they recognize what is already there, already given, waiting to be seen, to be taken up, enjoyed. What a waste to go through life surrounded by all the good gifts that God showers on me, "gently and generously" yet blind and deaf to his presence hidden in all things, human and nonhuman. As I learn not to take for granted, to wonder anew, I find that a constant attitude of gratitude is life-giving. In the face of such amazing grace and generosity, the only possible response must become that of continuing and ever-deepening praise.

NOTES

Introduction

1. It is essential to use this term and not to speak of the "Celtic Church," which can be misleading if it suggests that there ever was a Celtic Church as opposed to a "Roman Church." Any such idea would have been totally inimical to the Celtic people, who never regarded themselves as being in some different church, and for whom the Bishop of Rome always remained important.

2. See Patrick Barry OSB, *Saint Benedict and Christianity in England* (Ampleforth Abbey Press, 1995).

3. The six volumes of the *Carmina Gadelica,* songs, prayers, and blessings from the oral tradition of the western Highlands and islands of Scotland, were originally collected and edited by Alexander Carmichael at the end of the last century and published by the Scottish Academic Press as *Carmina Gadelica, Hymns and Incantations Orally Collected in the Highlands and Islands of Scotland and Translated into English.* There will be many subsequent references in the rest of the book to the *Carmina Gadelica,* since these poems, prayers, songs, and blessings (it is impossible to fit them into any neat categories) have been a source of enjoyment, inspiration, and practical prayer ever since I first discovered them. Although the six original volumes were published under a variety of editors between 1900 and 1928, in order to make them more easily accessible I edited them in 1988 as *Celtic Vision, Prayers and Blessings from the Outer Hebrides* (St. Bede's Publications, Petersham, Massachusetts). There is in addition a very short introduction *God Under*

My Roof (Paraclete Press). They have now been made easily available in a single volume, a new edition published in 1992 with a preface by John MacInnes from Floris Books, and have inspired the prolific output of David Adam, who has taken their format and produced modern versions which, however attractive, I feel lack much of the depth and the sense of harsh reality that make the original prayers so powerful. To sentimentalize or to sanitize is tempting, but it is a betrayal of this way of praying.

4. From a ninth-century Welsh poem, in Oliver Davies and Fiona Bowie, *Celtic Christian Spirituality, an Anthology of Medieval and Modern Sources* (Continuum), p. 27.

5. Thomas Merton, *Contemplation in a World of Action* (Image Books, 1973), p. 357.

6. This is one of the reasons I edited the translations by Helen Waddell of the stories of the friendships between the Desert Fathers and the Celtic saints and the wild creatures who played such an important role in their lives, *Beasts and Saints* (Eerdmans, 1996).

1 Journeying

1. Kuno Meyer (tr.), *Selections from Ancient Irish Poetry* (Constable, 1911, new ed., 1959), p. 100.

2. Charles Plummer, *Lives of the Irish Saints* (Oxford, 1922), II, p. 260, a reference which I owe to Brendan Lehane, *Early Celtic Christianity* (Constable, 1993), p. 71.

3. G. S. M. Walker (tr., ed.), *Sancti Columbani Opera*, Sermon VIII (Dublin, 1957), p. 97.

4. Plummer, *Lives*, II, p. 16.

5. See J. F. Webb, *Lives of the Saints* "The Old Irish Life of St. Columba," (New York, 1981), pp. 19–20.

6. Nora Chadwick, *Age of the Saints in the Early Celtic Church* (Oxford University Press, 1961), p. 64.

7. Eleanor Duckett, *The Wandering Saints* (Collins, 1959), pp. 25–6.

8. Davies and Bowie, *Anthology*, p. 37.

9. I owe this to Paul Pearson, "Celtic Monasticism as a Metaphor for Thomas Merton's Journey," *Hallel*, 19, 1994, pp. 50–7. The Merton poem that he quotes is from his *Collected Poems* (London, 1978), p. 201.

10. Duckett, *Wandering Saints*, p. 24.

11. *Carmina Gadelica*, III, p. 261.

12. Ibid., p. 275.

13. Ibid., p. 191.

14. Ibid., p. 195.

15. *Carmina Gadelica*, II, p. 321.

16. *Carmina Gadelica*, III, p. 247.

17. Ibid., p. 251.

18. Ibid., p. 255.

19. *Carmina Gadelica*, II, p. 171.

20. Douglas Hyde was in Ireland at the same time Alexander Carmichael was in Scotland, and we owe to him the songs and blessings that he also collected from the people whom he met as he traveled in Connacht. *Religious Songs of Connacht* (London, Dublin, 1906, reprinted with an introduction by Dominic Daly, Irish University Press, 1972).

21. *Carmina Gadelica*, III, p. 181.

22. *Carmina Gadelica*, II, pp. 158–9.

23. I owe these to two references to Alwyn Rees and Brinley Rees, *Celtic Heritage, Ancient Tradition in Ireland and Wales* (Thames and Hudson, 1994), p. 157.

24. "The deer's cry" was probably written in the eighth century. There are many translations, notably that of Mrs. Alexander in the last century. Here I have used a new one which I think brings out more of the original by Neil Dermott O'Donoghue, "St. Patrick's Breastplate," in James P. Mackey (ed.), *An Introduction to Celtic Christianity* (T & T Clark, 1989), pp. 45–64.

25. What I have just said here owes something to the final paragraph on p. 192 of Thomas Owen Clancy and Gilbert Markus, OP, *Iona, the Earliest Poetry of a Celtic Monastery* (Edinburgh University Press, 1995).

26. O'Donoghue in the article referred to in Note 24.

27. The Rule of St. Benedict continues to play a most important role in my life, and I have found that my discovery of the Celtic tradition has deepened and enriched what the Benedictine tradition has given me. See my *Seeking God, the Way of St. Benedict* and *A Life-Giving Way, a Commentary on the Rule of St. Benedict,* published by the Liturgical Press.

28. *Carmina Gadelica,* III, p. 207 (adapted so that it here becomes a personal prayer and one that fits in with the journey theme).

2 Image and Song

1. *Carmina Gadelica,* III, p. 3. Carmichael devotes pp. 16–23 of this volume to the subject of birth and baptism and has much interesting material. I have summarized a little of it in *Celtic Vision,* pp. 111–16.

2. *Carmina Gadelica,* I, pp. 232–3. I had delighted in this prayer for many years but I was given a greater fullness of

understanding by what Noel Dermott O'Donoghue has to say about it in *The Mountain Behind the Mountain* (T & T Clark, 1993), p. 48.

3. G.S.M. Walker (tr. and ed.), *Sancti Columbani Opera,* (Dublin, 1957), Sermon XII, pp. 111–13.

4. *Carmina Gadelica,* I, p. 35.

5. *Carmina Gadelica,* III, pp. 21–3.

6. Michael Maher (ed.), *Irish Spirituality* (Veritas Publications, 1981), p. 18.

7. Eoin de Bhaldraithe, "Obedience: The Doctrine of the Irish Monastic Rules," *Monastic Studies,* 14, 1983, p. 71.

8. Brendan Bradshaw, "Early Irish Christianity" in W. J. Shields (ed.), *The Churches, Ireland and the Irish* (Blackwell, 1989), p. 18.

9. Robin Flower, *The Irish Tradition* (Oxford University Press, 1948), p. 6. Alwyn Rees and Brinley Rees have much of interest to say on this subject in *Celtic Heritage.* They discuss how in pre-Christian literature the natural and the supernatural worlds intrude upon each other in a variety of ways. Between the two worlds is an interaction that is similar in many ways to the interaction between the conscious and the unconscious mind as described by modern psychologists, i.e., the ancient traditions and attitudes of mind have prepared the way for the Christian tradition.

10. I owe this to Ivor-Smith Cameron, *Pilgrimage, an Exploration into God* (Diocese of Southwark), p. 71.

3 The Trinity

1. Eleanor Hull, *The Poem Book of the Gael* (Chatto, 1912), p. 237, under the section "Religious Poems of the People," i.e., verses without attribution.

2. T. Ellis and J. H. Davies, *Gweithiau Morgan Llwyd* (University of Wales Press, 1899), Vol. i, p. 188.

3. I owe these ideas to Brendan Lehane, *Early Celtic Christianity*, p. 40.

4. *Carmina Gadelica*, III, p. 7.

5. Ibid., pp. 17–19.

6. Ibid., p. 137.

7. Hyde, *Religious Songs*, II, p. 39.

8. *Carmina Gadelica*, III, p. 93.

9. These ideas come from an article by Robert Culhane on the *Hymnus Dicat* in *Irish Ecclesiastical Record*, 1950.

10. J. Svoverffy, "The Altus Prosator and the Discovery of America," *Irish Ecclesiastical Record*, 1963, Vol. c, 5th series, p. 115.

11. Clancy and Markus, *Iona*, p. 45.

12. Diarmuid O'Laoghaire, "The Celtic Monk at Prayer," *Monastic Studies*, 14, 1983, p. 133.

13. James Carney (ed.), *The Poems of Blathmac, Son of Cu Brettan* (Irish Texts Society, 1966), vv. 196–7, and 191–5.

14. *Carmina Gadelica*, I, pp. 236–7.

15. Ibid., p. 311.

16. Hull, *Poem Book*, "Poem of Murdoch O'Daly," pp. 157–8.

4 Time

1. Lennox Barrow, *Irish Round Towers*, Irish Heritage series, (Eason & Son).

2. Eoin Neeson, *Poems from the Irish* (Mercier Press, 1967), p. 113.

3. *Abbey Psalter, the Book of Psalms Used by the Trappist Monks of Genesee Abbey* (Paulist Press, 1981).

4. Kuno Meyer, *Learning in Ireland in the Fifth Century and the Transmission of Letters* (Dublin, 1913), p. 18.

5. Kuno Meyer, *Four Old Irish Songs of Summer and Winter* (David Hutt, 1903), pp. 8–9.

6. *Carmina Gadelica*, III, pp. 306–7.

7. Ibid., p. 309.

8. Ibid., p. 287, from Isabel MacNeill, cottar of Barra.

9. Ibid., p. 275.

10. Ibid., p. 289.

11. Ibid., p. 291.

12. O'Donoghue, *The Mountain Behind the Mountain*.

13. *Carmina Gadelica*, I, p. 245. (I have omitted a final verse.)

14. Ibid., p. 247. (The full text is given in *Celtic Vision*, p. 531.)

15. Ibid., p. 22.

16. Ibid., p. 163.

17. Ibid., p. 291.

18. Ibid., p. 193.

5 The Presence of God

1. Hyde, *Religious Songs*, I, p. 3.

2. Leon Shenandoah, "Iroquois," in Steve Wall and Harvey Arden (eds.), *Meetings with Native American Spiritual Elders*, p. 104.

3. Hyde, *Religious Songs*, p. 172.

4. In this chapter I am trying not to duplicate what I have said elsewhere, notably in the opening chapter of *Every Earthly Blessing*, entitled "God's World," or in the article published in *Weavings*, "The Ordinary and the Extraordinary" in John Mogabgab (ed.), *Living with God in the World* (Upper Room Books, 1993), pp. 127–35.

5. *Carmina Gadelica*, I, p. vii.

6. *Carmina Gadelica*, III, p. 275.

7. Hull, *Poem Book*, p. xxxvii.

8. Hyde, *Religious Songs*, I, p. 3. Here I have changed the singular, man, since I am sure that it was common to both men and women.

9. *Carmina Gadelica*, I, p. 3.

10. Ibid., p. 5.

11. *Carmina Gadelica*, III, p. 33.

12. Ibid., p. 25.

13. *Carmina Gadelica*, I, p. 63.

14. Hyde, *Religious Songs*, II, p. 207.

15. *Carmina Gadelica*, III, p. 25.

16. Ibid., p. 27.

17. *Carmina Gadelica*, IV, p. 65.

18. Hyde, *Religious Songs*, II, p. 383.

19. Whitley Stokes (ed.), *Lives of the Saints from the Book of Lismore* (Clarendon Press, 1890), pp. 186–7.

20. *Carmina Gadelica*, IV, p. 87. Note the Irish form of the name Columba in this Scottish prayer which can only be evidence of the close connection between the two countries.

Here I have omitted the intervening verses which obviously were cheerful sounds to encourage˘ the work, "Stillim! Steoilim! Strichim! Streochim!"

21. Hyde, *Religious Songs*, II, p. 73.

22. See the introduction, An Tath. Uinseann OCSO, *Urnaithe Na Ngael, Traditional Irish Prayers, Grace Before and After Meals* (1975), a collection of nearly sixty of these prayers, with translation from the Gaelic and short commentary.

23. Hull, *Poem Book*, p. 236 (traditional).

24. *Carmina Gadelica*, I, p. 305.

25. *Carmina Gadelica*, IV, pp. 87–8.

26. *Carmina Gadelica*, I, p. 311.

27. Ibid., p. 297.

28. Ibid., p. 27.

29. Ibid., p. 283.

30. Ibid., p. 329.

31. *Carmina Gadelica*, III, p. 178.

32. Ibid., p. 181.

33. Hyde, *Religious Songs*, II, p. 47. A number of these smooring prayers are to be found in *Carmina Gadelica*, I, pp. 237–43.

34. Donn Byrne, *The Power of the Dog* (Penguin, 1947), p. 16.

35. *Carmina Gadelica*, I, p. 67.

36. Ibid., p. 83.

6 The Solitary

1. Thomas Merton (tr.), *The Wisdom of the Desert, Sayings from the Desert Fathers of the Fourth Century* (Sheldon Press, 1961), XIII, p. 30.

2. That wonderful small phrase "rinsed eyes" was used recently about Thomas Merton, and I feel that it applies to these earlier hermits too. Merton has in our own lifetime written much about the hermit life that he was himself allowed to live in his small hut in the woods outside the Cistercian monastery of Gethsemani in Kentucky. Because he stands back in non-attachment, never wanting to possess, to organize, to control a world that he sees as a gift, he can, as it were, let each individual thing have its own voice. In Thomas Merton's case we can see how he took time with his photographs, and how in his hands the camera became a contemplative instrument, each thing approached with gentleness, respecting its uniqueness. I have discussed this in *A Seven Day Journey with Thomas Merton* (Servant Publications).

3. Kenneth Jackson, *Studies in Early Celtic Nature Poetry* (Cambridge University Press, 1935).

4. Kenneth Jackson, *A Celtic Miscellany, Translations from the Celtic Literatures* (Routledge & Kegan Paul, 1951), pp. 183, 63.

5. This is an extract from that long and famous hermit poem which takes the shape of a fictional dialogue between King Guaire of Connacht (d. *c.* 663) and his half brother, the hermit Marvan. I have taken this translation from Ludwig Bieler, *Ireland: Harbinger of the Middle Ages* (Oxford University Press, 1963).

6. Gerard Murphy (ed.), *Early Irish Lyrics, Eighth to Twelfth Century* (Oxford University Press, 1956), pp. 11–19 (shortened).

7. For an alternative translation see David Greene and Frank O'Connor (eds.), *A Golden Treasury of Irish Poetry* A.D. 600–1200 (Macmillan, 1967), p. 150.

8. Clancy and Markus, *Iona,* p. 90, where we are given a refreshingly acerbic assessment of early Irish nature poetry.

9. Jackson, *Studies,* pp. 105–6.

10. Clancy and Markus, *Iona,* p. 1.

11. *Preoccupations. Selected Prose 1968–1978* (Faber, 1980), p. 189.

12. Flower, *Irish Tradition,* p. 4.

13. Clancy and Markus, *Iona,* p. 90.

14. Jackson, *Studies,* pp. 9–10. Although it is attributed to St. Columba it is likely that this poem dates from the twelfth century. I have omitted the three final verses.

15. Murphy (ed.), *Early Irish Lyrics,* pp. 11–19; also in A. M. Allchin and Esther de Waal (eds.) *Daily Readings from Prayers and Praises in the Celtic Tradition* (Templegate).

16. O'Loaghaire, "The Celtic Monk at Prayer."

17. Waddell, *Beasts and Saints,* where the introduction explores this further.

18. Mary Tordiss, O.P. (ed.), *At Home in the World, the Letters of Thomas Merton and Rosemary Radford Reuther* (Orbis, 1995), pp. 35–6.

19. Waddell, *Beasts and Saints,* pp. 23–6.

20. A. M. Allchin, *Pennant Melangell, Place of Pilgrimage* (Gwasg Santes Melangell, 1994), p. 5.

21. Ibid. I have written about this before in the chapter "Common Creation" in *Every Earthly Blessing* and in the introduction to the new edition of *Beasts and Saints.*

22. Sr. Benedicta Ward, SLG, *The Spirituality of St. Cuthbert* (Fairacres, 1992), p. 10.

23. Waddell, *Beasts and Saints,* p. 62.

7 Dark Forces

1. *An Interview with Dennis Potter* by Melvyn Bragg, broadcast on April 5, 1994, in England, on Channel 4 Television.

2. Rev. George MacLeod, *The Whole Earth Shall Cry Glory,* Iona Prayers (Wild Goose, 1985), p. 8.

3. Patrick Thomas, A *Candle in the Darkness: Celtic Spirituality from Wales* (Gomer Press, 1993), p. 12.

4. "Fires on Llyn," *Selected Poems* (Carcanet, 1985). I am grateful to Gillian Clarke for permission to quote these lines.

5. Ibid.

6. This is taken from a small pamphlet, *A Way to God for Today,* compiled by Cynthia and Saunders Davies for the Llandaff Diocesan Renewal Service Team.

7. Davies and Bowie, *Anthology,* pp. 31–2.

8. Clancy and Markus, *Iona,* p. 183.

9. Murphy (ed.), *Early Irish Lyrics,* pp. 51–3. The full text is given in *A World Made Whole,* p. 102.

10. *Saltair na Ramm,* lines 1491–1530.

11. Again the full text can be found in *Every Earthly Blessing,* p. 103.

12. Davies and Bowie, *Anthology,* p. 34.

13. Again the whole poem is to be found in *Every Earthly Blessing,* p. 104.

14. I have written about it briefly in Robert Llewellyn (ed.), *Circles of Silence* (Darton, Longman & Todd, 1994), pp. 54–6.

15. Kenneth Jackson, *Studies in Celtic Nature Poetry* (Cambridge University Press, 1935), pp. 105–6.

16. Charles Plummer, *Irish Litanies* (London, Henry Bradshaw Society, 1925), "Litany of the Saviour," p. 21.

17. Charles Plummer, *Lives of the Irish Saints* (Clarendon Press, 1922), II, p. 5.

18. Davies and Bowie, *Anthology*, p. 45.

19. Plummer, *Lives*, p. 79.

20. L. Bieler, *Irish Penitentials* (Dublin Institute for Advanced Studies, 1963).

21. See Ed Sellner, "A Common Dwelling: Soul Friendship in Early Celtic Monasticism," *Cistercian Studies Quarterly*, Vol. 29, 1995, p. 6.

22. Whitley Stokes (ed.), *The Martyrology of Oengus the Culdee* (London, 1905), p. 65.

23. Ibid., pp. 161, 267.

24. Ibid., p. 144. See also E. J. Gwynn and W. J. Purton, "The Monastery of Tallaght," *Proceedings of the Royal Irish Academy*, 1911, XXIX, C, pp. 135–6.

8 The Cross

1. Gwenallt, *Eples* (Gomer Press, 1951), pp. 63–4. The full poem is to be found in *Daily Readings from Prayers and Praises in the Celtic Tradition*.

2. *Thomas, Candle*, pp. 15, 136.

3. Ibid., p. 78.

4. O'Donoghue, *The Mountain Behind the Mountain,* p. 3.

5. My ideas on this were much helped by a short discussion on Cistercian art (which is also nonrepresentational and connected with liturgical use) by Meredith Parsons Lillich in *The Abbey Psalter* (The Paulist Press, 1981).

6. Brendan Lehane, who understands the Irish imagination so well, has much to say that is interesting here, especially about the Irish fascination with significant numbers, three in particular, in *Early Celtic Christianity,* p. 40.

7. Hilary Richardson, "Number and Symbol in Early Christian Art," *Journal of the Royal Society of Antiquaries of Ireland,* 1984, 114, pp. 28–47; and "Celtic art," in James Mackey (ed.), *Introduction to Celtic Christianity,* pp. 359–86.

8. Eoin de Bhaldraithe, *The High Crosses of Moone and Castlerdermot, a Guided Tour* (privately published at Bolton Abbey, Ireland). I am grateful to the author for permission to quote from this most useful discussion of the crosses.

9. Hyde, *Religious Songs,* II, p. 35.

10. Prayer of Protection, *Carmina Gadelica,* III, p. 109.

11. Hyde, *Religious Songs,* II, p. 395. The full text can be found in *Every Earthly Blessing,* p. 128.

12. Thomas, *Candle,* p. 82.

13. *Carmina Gadelica,* II, pp. 104–5.

14. Hull, *Poem Book,* pp. 254–5.

15. *The Private Devotions of the Welsh in Days Gone By* (Foulkes, 1898), p. 28. I owe this reference to Anthony Packer, "Medieval Welsh Spirituality," a paper given in Cardiff in May 1995 on pilgrimages in the Welsh spiritual tradition.

16. Ibid., p. 35.

17. Carney (ed.), *Poems of Blathmac.*

18. Preface to Stokes (ed.), *Lives,* p. v.

19. Murphy (ed.), *Early Irish Lyrics,* p. 33, and O'Laoghaire, "The Celtic Monk at Prayer," p. 131.

20. Daphne Pochin Mould, *Irish Saints* (Burns & Oates, 1964), p. 182.

21. Waddell, *Beasts and Saints,* p. 121.

22. Ambrosian Library at Milan, quoted in O'Laoghaire, "The Celtic Monk at Prayer," p. 130.

23. *Carmina Gadelica,* III, p. 71.

24. Ibid., p. 83.

25. *Carmina Gadelica,* I, p. 67.

26. Ibid., 94. (The full version can be found in *Celtic Vision,* p. 97.)

27. *Carmina Gadelica,* III, p. 102; II, p. 240.

28. *Carmina Gadelica,* III, p. 103.

29. Pochin Mould, *Irish Saints,* pp. 235–6.

30. *Carmina Gadelica,* III, pp. 73–5.

31. *Carmina Gadelica,* I, p. 77.

9 The Saints

1. It reminds me of the young African priest whom I mentioned on p. 27 talking about how on our journey in life we become more and more close to others, so that it is essentially a corporate, shared experience. That is why I think that people who come out of traditional African society can appreciate the Celtic tradition, for they accept as entirely

natural that those who have died, whom they call the "living dead," continue to play an important part in their lives.

2. D. A. Binchy, *Early Irish Society*, M. Dillon (ed.), (Dublin, 1954), p. 54.

3. Kathleen Hughes, "Sanctity and Secularity in the Early Irish Church," *Studies in Church History*, D. Baker (ed.) (Cambridge University Press, 1973), p. 10.

4. Davies and Bowie, *Anthology*, pp. 38–9.

5. *Carmina Gadelica*, I, p. 165ff.

6. I owe this to E. G. Bowen, *The Settlements of the Celtic Saints in Wales* (University of Wales Press, 1956), p. 4. Ciaran O'Sabhaois says that there are 3,025 places beginning with "Kil" in Ireland, of which fifty-two are dedicated to St. Brigid and twenty-two to St. Patrick. See his article in *Cistercian Studies Quarterly*, 10, 1975.

7. *Aristocracy of Soul, Patrick of Ireland* (Darton, Longman & Todd, 1987), p. 80.

8. See Dorothy Ann Bray, "The Making of a Hero," *Monastic Studies*, 14, p. 153. She is referring to Peter Brown, *The Cult of the Saints, Its Rise and Function in a Latin Christianity* (London, 1981), pp. 5–6.

9. Jackson, *Celtic Miscellany*, pp. 312–13. Unknown author, possibly ninth century.

10. Cogitosus's "Life of St. Brigid" in *Patrologia Latina*, pp. 72, 75.

11. Ibid., p. 71.

12. A. W. Wade-Evans, *Vitae Sanctorum* (University of Wales, 1944), p. 267.

13. *Carmina Gadelica*, I, p. 165.

14. Waddell, *Beasts and Saints*, pp. 127–30.

15. Ibid., pp. 91–6.

16. Richard Sharpe (tr.), *Adomnan of Iona, Life of St. Columba* (Penguin, 1995), p. 200, pp. 228–30.

17. The earliest surviving texts are from the early tenth century, though it was clearly based on oral tradition and probably written in the ninth century. More than 120 Latin manuscripts survive, for it was one of the most popular of all legends in the early Middle Ages, and widely translated into both romance and Germanic vernacular.

18. The voyage of Brendan was the most famous of the *immrama* voyages to "other-world" islands. It is given in Alwyn Rees and Brindley Rees, *Celtic Heritage,* pp. 314–16. These are journeys into another dimension, journeys between this world and the next, the only journey of any real significance. As Nora Chadwick recognizes, Celtic writing is here in step with the literature the world over: "In Asia, in Polynesia, even in Africa, man's chief intellectual preoccupations and speculations are with spiritual adventure . . . the lonely pioneering of the soul . . . and the defeat or success of its quest forms the principal theme in the oral literature of the Old World," *Poetry and Prophecy* (Cambridge University Press, 1942), p. 92.

19. Naomi Stone (ed.), *A Vow of Conversation* (The Lamp Press, 1988), p. 71. See also Cynthea Bourgeault's most valuable article, where she says that this must be the "organisational principle" from which we start, "Navigation of St. Brendan," *Monastic Studies,* 14, 1983, pp. 109–22.

20. Stokes (ed.), *Martyrology,* pp. 17, 277, 288.

21. K. Jackson, "The Vision of Adhamhnan," *Celtic Miscellany,* p. 290ff.

22. *Peig. The Autobiography of Peig Sayers of the Great Blasket Island,* Bryan MacMahon (tr.) (Talbot Press, 1974).

23. Gwenallt, *Eples,* pp. 63–4.

10 Praise

1. G. Murphy, *Early Irish Lyrics* (Oxford University Press, 1956), p. 4.

2. O'Laoghaire, "The Celtic Monk at Prayer," p. 134, where he gives the full reference in Note 27.

3. Thomas, *Candle,* pp. 61–2, to whom I also owe the comments here. The poem is probably ninth century. The translation is by Sir Ifor Williams, *Beginnings in Welsh Poetry* (University of Wales Press, 1972), p. 102. A fuller version and an alternative translation will be found in Davies and Bowie, *Anthology,* pp. 27–8.

4. Davies and Bowie, *Anthology,* pp. 54–6.

5. Thomas, *Candle,* p. 139.

6. I have used here the translation that is found in Joseph P. Clancy, *The Earliest Welsh Poetry* (Macmillan, 1970), p. 113, which I used in *Daily Readings from Prayers and Praises in the Celtic Tradition* (Templegate).

7. Davies and Bowie, *Anthology,* pp. 31–2, to whom I also owe the comments on this poem.

8. Clancy and Markus, *Iona,* pp. 45–53.

9. Thomas Jones, "The Mistle Thrush" in Davies and Bowie, *Anthology,* pp. 56–7.

10. *Journal of a Solitude* (W. W. Norton & Co, 1977), p. 99.

11. Meyer, *Four Old Irish Songs,* pp. 9ff. I have given only a selection of verses here.

12. A. M. Allchin, *Praise Above All* (University of Wales Press, 1991), p. 37.

13. This is the first half of the poem only. Cynthia and Saunders Davies (eds.), *Euros Bowen, Priest-poet* (Church in Wales Publications, 1993), p. 143.

14. Jackson, *Studies in Early Celtic Nature Poetry*, pp. 108–9. The poem is eighth or ninth century.

15. I owe this information to Sr. Helen Colomba, SLG, of Fairacres, Oxford, and her interest in traditional Scottish songs.

16. *Carmina Gadelica*, III, p. 25. It is quoted in *Celtic Vision*, p. 5.

17. Ibid., p. 31.

18. Ibid., p. 29.

19. *Carmina Gadelica*, II, pp. 41–7 (shortened). The full version is to be found in *Celtic Vision*, pp. 20–3.

20. *Carmina Gadelica*, III, pp. 54–61 (shortened).

21. I owe this quotation to A. M. Allchin, *Praise Above All*, p. 3. He has taken it from David Jones, *Epoch and Artist* (London, 1959), p. 281.

22. *"Cantemus in omni die,"* a hymn to Our Lady written around 700 by a scholarly monk of Iona, in Clancy and Markus, *Iona*, p. 183.

23. Sharpe, *Adomnan*, p. 228.

24. James Carney, *Medieval Irish Lyrics*, p. 74. But I owe this reference to Martin McNamara, "The Psalter in Early Irish Monastic Spirituality," *Monastic Studies*, 14, p. 186.

25. Plummer, *Lives*, I, p. 172.

26. Duckett, *Wandering Saints*, p. 271.

27. Henri J. M. Nouwen, *The Genesee Diary, Report from a Trappist Monastery* (Image Books, Doubleday, 1976), entry under Friday, August 2.

28. Thomas Merton, *Praying the Psalms* (Liturgical Press, 1956), p. 7, 10–11.

29. Davies and Bowie, *Anthology*, p. 29.

INDEX

p. 27
p. 156 - prayer
p. 42 Wisdom, peace, purity